Lloyd
9/2007

TEN POINTS

TEN POINTS

BILL STRICKLAND

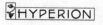

NEW YORK

Library of Congress Cataloging-in-Publication Data

Ten points / Bill Strickland.
     p. cm.
     ISBN-10: 1-4013-0258-0
     ISBN-13: 978-1-4013-0258-0
     1. Strickland, Bill, 1964–. 2. Cycling—United States—Anecdotes. 3. Cyclists—United
     States—Biography. I. Title.
     GV1051.S87 A3 2007
     796.6092 B 22

                                                                    2006046904

Hyperion books are available for special promotions and premiums. For details
contact Michael Rentas, Assistant Director, Inventory Operations, Hyperion, 77 West
66th Street, 12th floor, New York, New York 10023, or call 212-456-0133.

Design by Paul Perlow

FIRST EDITION

10 9 8 7 6 5 4 3 2 1

For Natalie,
because I promised you ten points

Ever tried. Ever failed. No matter. Try again.
Fail again. Fail better.
—SAMUEL BECKETT

Acknowledgments & A Note About Truth

This story is immeasurably indebted to the talents of my first readers: Peter Flax, the best line editor I know; Jeremy Katz, the first person who told me my quest was a book; Steve Madden, the editor who convinced me I should write about my family (for a *Bicycling* magazine article that contained the seed of this book); and Nelson Pena, who read the story maybe even more times than I did, and who saved the ending. My agent, David Black, who stuck with me even though I could not look him in the eye the first time I tried to describe the story, has many gifts; the greatest is his ability to believe. Leslie Wells, my editor, pushed the story in directions I hadn't anticipated nor could have found on my own. The fresh eyes of Miriam Wenger fixed some key narrative breakdowns. And Bill Strachan bought the thing in the first place—thanks.

I'd also like to thank those who raced the Thursday Night Crit during the 2004 season, especially those who became, to varying degrees, my friends on the road or just outright friends: Ken Bacher, Bruce Donaghy, Andy Kuklis, Ray Ignosh, Jack Simes, and, of course, Paul Pearson, the Animal.

* * *

Because it was important not only to the integrity of the story, but also to what I needed to accomplish, I wrote the story of *Ten Points* with as much honesty and accuracy as I could.

The depictions of my father, and the incidents of my childhood, are as authentic in detail and sequence as my recall allows, and were verified against the remembrances of my mother and sister. Certain sections of dialogue are word for word, like a transcript; they are burned into my memory. Other verbal exchanges are re-created based on what I know of each person's phrasing and vocabulary, and by drawing on later situations in our lives together, from which I could remember specifics of speech. In many instances, my mother and, to a lesser extent, my sister and my cousin Gary Strickland (the son of my father's brother, Gary) contributed or corrected details that had eluded me or become garbled in my memory—from the color of a chair in our living room to the name of the motorcycle gang my uncle belonged to. For wading through such personally painful material in the service of fact-checking, and for surviving, I cannot thank them enough. The history of my extended family is recounted true to the way it was always told to me; however, some members of my family who read the book before publication disagree with my characterization, in particular the depiction of my grandfather, which, it should be noted, by circumstance relies solely on statements my father made to me rather than on personal experience.

I am aware that my experience of racing was filtered through an oxygen-starved mind. While the emotional and physical tolls of each criterium are solely my interpretation—

and surely not representative of the overall race in the way that a newspaper sports report would be—thanks to access to the score sheets and the records kept by Chip Berezny and the other officials, and to objective, from-the-sideline summaries supplied all season long by Peter Flax and Beth, the depictions of who raced and who scored each week are accurate. You can find scores, stats, and more information on that season and others at lehighwheelmen.org.

Every bicycle racer mentioned is a real person with a real name (or real nickname). For some other characters throughout the book, names have been omitted or changed, as have some identifying attributes, to protect their privacy and shield them from any misinterpretations I may have made while trying to capture their characters—although I believe the spirit of each remains true to my perception. And because so many of my early readers asked: As far as my mother and I can determine, Charlie Mexico was the only name by which that character was known to our family and friends. He's real.

Finally, for being with me through all of this—reading draft after draft as well as living it year after year—and for understanding that disclosing so much personal detail strengthened the story, and for rescuing me from such inaccuracies as claiming that a steer could give birth to a calf, and for saving our marriage and, in some way no doubt, the life of our daughter, I will spend the rest of my heartbeats, and perhaps more, trying to thank Beth.

TEN POINTS

one

SHE WAS SHIMMYING AROUND ON THE TOILET THERE IN
her bathroom, my daughter, and swinging her feet against me
as I sat on the floor, still sweaty in my cycling clothes. I was
propped back on my arms, my legs stretched out in front of
me, and as Natalie said, "Hold me," she ticked her feet against
the left side of my chest twice.

She'd already gotten dressed for pre-K, in a red sweater and,
crumpled around her feet, kitten underpants and blue jeans
with flowers embroidered on the cuffs. Nat has Beth's nose
and lips and cheeks and ears, and also my wife's way of setting
her face whether in joy or sorrow. Her blue eyes are hers
alone, but there's something of me in them—not the color or
shape, but a thing that dances in and out of sight. It flitted between us now.

"Dadda, hold me," she said, as her feet whapped me twice
more. Under the black spandex streaked with snot and smears

1

of the banana that had been my rolling breakfast, my leg muscles squirmed like something trapped inside me. My rib cage registered two more thumps.

Natalie's caramel-blonde hair, curled in where it ended along the lines of her chin, swayed in time with her legs. I sat up and leaned toward her and put my hands on her shoulders, then back and down, across the pointy angles of her shoulder blades, so sharp on her they always seemed to me like wings about to bud. She lay her head against me.

This ritual was a remnant from potty training, when Natalie sometimes perched on the toilet for twenty minutes trying to poop or pee, never sure which she might do, or when she might start, or if she was finished. Beth and I had fallen into a habit of sitting in front of her, talking, telling her stories, wrapping our arms around her back. Our most long, searching, complex discussions happened this way: how the universe started, "what stuff is made of" (it had taken me ten minutes to figure out she was talking about matter and atoms, rather than wood or steel), why people die, why the various disciplines Beth and I meted out did not feel fair. Now that she was five, Natalie didn't really need to do this anymore, but she was hanging onto the practice and, in truth, so was I. It was the same instinct that, since she'd started to pronounce almost all of her words correctly, made me hoard the few she still said slightly, adorably wrong: napkim, darkeness, bemember.

"Listen," Natalie said, talking against my shoulder. "You are smelly but this is important. I have been thinking."

"Not again," I said.

"For real life. You told Steak that getting ten points is impossible."

Steak, who worked with me and was one of my best friends, had been hanging out after a ride a few days ago and we'd been obsessing once again over my chances in the bicycle race that had come to dominate our conversations: the Thursday Night Criterium. "For me, at least, it is impossible," I told Natalie. "That's kind of the idea."

"But, Daddy, you're so so so fast."

"There are a lot of people at the Crit faster than me, Riff." This was one of several nicknames I'd given Natalie that had stuck, this one shortened from T-o-riffic, which was shortened from Terrifico, which sometimes became Turd-o-riffic when she was pestering me or Beth. "One of them was the champion of the entire world, and won a gold medal at the Olympics. Some of them are legends. Some are pros."

"I know." Her voice came to me as a vibration through my shoulder as much as a sound. "You're not a champion, are you?"

"No," I said. "I'm an editor." I was a thirty-nine-year-old desk jockey, but as I sat in the bathroom with my daughter on that morning in early April, I had pedaled myself into the best shape of my life. I weighed 153 pounds, chiseled down from a 175 that no one except my new acquaintances—bicycle racers—would have described as fat. My resting heart rate was somewhere in the mid-fifties and, when I needed to, I could hammer along at more than 190 beats per minute for a ludicrous length of time. My body-fat percentage was about to dip under double digits. Lab tests I would take later that season would put me in the 90th percentiles for all men my age in measurements such as strength, flexibility, and aerobic capacity. Nowhere near enough.

"So what is the truth?" asked Natalie. "If you believe you can do it, is it really impossible or really possible?"

I leaned back and stared at her.

The truth was that there was no way I was going to be able to outsprint the real racers enough times to score ten points in the season-long series of weekly races, which was exactly the reason I needed to do it. The truth was that I never told anyone the truth about my quest. Not Steak or my other friends, not Natalie, not even Beth. When anyone I knew or met heard about what I was trying to do, they would say things such as "You're crazy," or "That's . . . interesting." Sometimes they asked questions I could give specific answers to: "How fast do you go?" or "Are there many crashes?" But inevitably, no matter who I was talking to, we got to the same question: Why?

I had no way to fully explain why I was throwing myself under the wheels of a pack of world-class cyclists, so I told people something that was true, but not all of the truth: The previous October, Natalie had made a spontaneous, childish wish that I would score ten points, and I had seized on the idea as a chance to show her that through work, and will, and willingness to sacrifice, dreams could come true. In a single year, I thought I could become not just living but lifelong proof that you should ask much, and expect much, of people you love.

"Hold me tighter," Natalie said. She tensed, and the water made a plopping sound and she said, "I'm pooping." I held her. I could feel her tiny spine shifting under my fingers. And, through the depth of her chest, her heart beating. A new, ripe, nearly sweet odor wafted through the room.

"I'm done," she announced.

"Wipe."

"Daddy—"

"Wipe," I said. "You need to start doing it, Boo."

"I know I wipe. I was going to say do you bemember my soul is a banana?"

"Yeah," I said. "Mine too. All of ours."

A few weeks earlier, I'd used a piece of fruit to explain the concept of a soul to Natalie. One of her cats, Jasper, had caught and killed a vole, and left it on our porch, and she wanted to know everything about death. She seemed most mortified that we bury or burn our dead. I told her that we are souls, not bodies.

We'd been having breakfast and, inspired, I plucked a banana from the bunch on the counter.

"What's this?" I asked.

"Banana."

I stripped off the skin, and tossed the peel off to the side. I held the banana back up between us again.

"Now," I said, "what's this?"

"Daddy. Why do you keep asking me what a banana is?"

"This is what I'm saying: When the banana loses its peel, it's still a banana, right? Our souls are like the banana. Our bodies are like the peel."

She'd cocked her head, and reached out and taken the fruit from my hand.

In the bathroom, frowning, Natalie said, "We're a banana when we have our body on."

I nodded.

"And we're a banana if our peel dies."

I nodded. "You got it."

"Daddy." My daughter, sitting on the toilet, looked into

me, and the thing flitted in her eyes. She said, "Daddy, who eats our souls?"

Before I reached my hand out and noticed that I still had my black, half-fingered cycling glove on and that it looked like some kind of paw against my daughter's tiny head, and before I laid my palm against the side of that fragile head anyway and gave the right answer, my breath caught.

"No one's going to eat your soul," I said.

A long time ago, a monster had eaten mine. But I was going to get it back. "No one's ever going to eat your soul," I promised. All I had to do was score ten points.

two

I HAD TO SCORE TEN POINTS.

When Beth and I were still living in that first small home we'd bought, the one where the baby we'd seen in fuzzy black-and-white ultrasound images and already nicknamed Squeezy was going to live in a nursery over the garage, and when our combined salaries were less than I'd be making in a few years, and when all of that had felt romantic rather than bleak until our first child died before getting a chance to live, we got into one more argument about nothing.

In the smoothest of times, having been married only five years or so, Beth and I were still at that stage when a disagreement about something like how to cook spaghetti could turn into an ultimatum about our future. With neither of us able to find a way out of our own grief, let alone reach through the other's, the fact that we were in love had come to feel like some kind of constant affront.

We were faced off against each other in the bedroom hallway that day. Beth's eyes, which could be green like grass or like emeralds, were hard and sharp. She was around five-foot-two, nearly seven inches shorter than me, yet had a way sometimes of making me feel she was looking straight into my eyes rather than up at me. It was the same characteristic that, though she barely nudged the scale over 100 and in certain clothes wore a size zero, let her stand stocky when she wanted to. When I admired some part of her without her knowing—studying the fine mesh her fingers made against the back of a book she was reading, or becoming fixated on the sweep of her collarbone as she hovered over me in bed—her every physical aspect appeared slender. But as a body, she was formidable.

As we argued that day, though, her mouth kept faltering, degenerating into a kind of bleary smear across her face. She wailed, "I'm just so tired of this chaos," pivoted to the left, and slammed her palm against the closet door. There was the hollow smack of her flesh, and a dull clink from a ring on her finger.

The sound lifted something inside me, sick and thrilling, as if I'd just heard the last pull of the chain at the top of a roller-coaster climb. I swallowed down hard against the terrifying rapture that was rising through me, trying to arrest it. "You don't know chaos," I said, meaning it not as an accusation, but an explanation. I twisted around and banged the door with the side of my foot. I looked at Beth, then slammed my right elbow against the thin, hollow-core veneer. There was a shallow dent. My arm hurt. I cocked my foot backward, then smashed the toe of my shoe through the light brown surface. I wrenched my foot out, stepped back, paused, then kicked again. There was a splintering sound. The bottom third of the door caved in, clutching at my foot. Beth was backing down the hallway, her eyes wide.

For one awful instant, I had a thought I've never been able to forgive myself for. I was grateful that we'd lost Squeezy, that no child would be forced to witness the dark holes I could open.

three

I WAS NEVER GOING TO SCORE TEN POINTS.

On the last Thursday in April, I clicked into the pedals of my $5,000 carbon bicycle and rolled away from my $1,000 pickup truck toward my weekly cremation at the Thursday Night Crit. Since the season had started, on the first Thursday of that month, every race had been the same. The inferno of color and sound and spit and sweat and swirling legs that raged across 50 feet of black asphalt every second would consume me well before half of the hour-long competition was over. From the sidelines, where Beth and Natalie had watched each race, my ritual incineration must not have looked like much. Each time, as the pack of fifty or more bicycles streamed through the tenth lap or so, I would be sifted wobbly and ashen out of the back, then coast into the grass beside the race course. My lips would be stuck together, crusted white at the corners. I'd twist my left foot out away from the bike to release my cleated shoe from the pedal, then plant the foot in the grass and sit my right thigh down across the top tube of the bike. The two wheels and my leg made a stable tripod. I'd collapse onto the scaffolding of myself, close my eyes, and hang my head over the handlebar. I imagined that my sputtering failures must have been like watching a candle burn—not much to it, unless you're the candle.

This week, I had showed up thirty minutes earlier to see if more warm-up laps could save me. I pedaled up onto a sidewalk, weaved around a boy pumping a training-wheel bike hard at his mom's heels, then turned onto a narrow, paved path shaded by overhanging trees. From there, I steered onto the race course.

"Whoa!" yelled a voice behind me. There was the sharp, high hiss of rubber brake pads against the aluminum sidewalls of wheels. "Watch it!"

I jerked—one of those full-body conniptions you make when you startle yourself just before falling asleep. My back wheel fishtailed, and the display of the heart-rate monitor mounted on my handlebar flared from 90 to 135.

The Animal rode up beside me.

Paul Pearson, the Animal, had earned his nickname over thirty-six years of racing, competing on two wheels nearly as long as I'd been alive. He was renowned for relentless, rabid attacks that forced others to chase him until they puked or quit. At forty-eight now, he'd retired from pro racing and had lost a mile or two per hour off his top speed. But even with diminishing fitness, his canniness kept him fast and dangerous. He was the unofficial boss of the Thursday Night Crit. And I'd cut him off.

The Animal put a hand on my shoulder as we rolled along. The nickname was apt. There was something wolfish about him, a quality projected not quite from his facial structure but in the accumulation of the uncountable, subtle gestures that communicate character. He wore a gray-streaked moustache, like someone from my dad's era, under a modern high-schooler's disheveled haircut. There was no way to figure the guy out.

We knew each other a little, from times we'd stopped at the same coffee shop, or passed each other out on the road. He pushed me a few inches to the side with his hand and said, "What are you doing out here?"

"Riding," was the only word that would drop from my brain to my mouth. I cringed, while trying to push out against my skin so maybe the Animal wouldn't notice. I waited for him to butt his head into mine, to drive me down to the asphalt for being a smartass.

He said, "Ha—yeah. I don't think you can call what we're doing racing at this time of year."

The Animal thought I was being humble. I moved my hands from the brake hoods to the tops of the handlebar, to show how at ease I was. I rolled my shoulders to display how thoroughly I was relaxing, and got ready to lay down some pre-Crit chatter with my good racing friend, the dangerous and dominating Animal. He rode off.

By an accident of geography, I am surrounded by elite cyclists. My home in Emmaus, Pennsylvania, about an hour north of Philadelphia, is just six miles from the Lehigh Valley Velodrome, a concrete oval, 333 meters around, that is not only the top bicycle racing track in this country but one of the best in the world; it attracts some of the sport's fastest, fittest, most powerful riders, who live in the region during race season. Go out for a ride in the Lehigh Valley and you might find yourself swarmed by a pack that includes three or four Olympians; national champions from the U.S., Australia, Argentina, England, Germany, New Zealand, Finland, and a few other countries; a squad or two of pro racers visiting friends or barnstorming through on their way to events out West; a few grizzled legends whose legs still defy their years; and teenage prodigies who in two or three decades will become legends themselves.

Every Thursday evening from early spring through late fall, these racers gather in a park across the street from the velodrome. The park has a sandbox, a nature trail, some stone benches, and a gazebo, but its dominant feature is a curvy, one-mile loop of asphalt built as a walking, skating, and family cycling circuit. Once a week, the loop is closed to the public for the running of the Thursday Night Criterium.

Crits, as they're called, are staged on loops that are usually about a mile long, at speeds ranging from 18 to 42 miles per hour. Some are based solely on finish order—the first three riders across the line on the last lap win; others, like the one I was racing, award points at regular intervals and, at the end, whoever has the greatest total wins. In the 30-lap, 30-mile Thursday Night Crit, we sprint for points every three laps; on each of those important laps—the 27th, the 24th, the 21st, etc.—the first rider across the finish line earns 5 points, the second rider 3 points, the third rider 2, and the fourth gets 1.

Only bragging rights are at stake on Thursdays—there are no cash or prizes, except a free pizza at the end of the month for the person with the highest score. For amateurs like me, the real reward is the Crit itself. Racing it is like getting to stand at home plate in Yankee Stadium and take a few cuts at a major leaguer's fastball. Non-pro cyclists are typically segregated into their own competitions but, because the organizer classified the Thursday Night Crit as "open," any amateur bike racer—that is, anyone who's met the stringent criteria of simply paying for a license—can line up behind the real thing and try to hang on.

There aren't many of us amateurs around. In the U.S., out of 22 million bike owners, various surveys and studies estimate that about 8 million of those are what's called "enthusiasts," who ride at least twice a week. Out of those 8 million committed cyclists, just about 32,000 own racing licenses. In one sense, the barrier to becoming a racer is laughably low: Go to the Web site of USA Cycling, charge $50 to your credit card, print out a license, and you can race that same day. But in reality, there are so few amateur racers—about four-tenths of 1 percent of those 8 million cycling fanatics—because the requirements are not so much exclusive as excruciating.

Bicycle road racing is unlike other amateur pursuits, such as softball or bowling or even running 5Ks, where you can be mediocre or even lousy but still participate. In a bike race, once you have dropped from the pack, you get pulled out of the event by officials—humiliated as well as depleted. And most beginners are left behind within minutes, if not seconds.

To merely hang with the pack at the Category 5 level, the lowest and easiest class of competition, a typical amateur trains around 200 miles a week, swapping television, books, parties, and most other leisure pursuits for riding time and as much restorative sleep as possible. You have to be willing to crash, especially amid the inexperienced and unskilled Cat 5 pack, where it's never a surprise to hear that someone broke a collarbone, a wrist, a leg, or their bike—and you'd almost rather bang up the body than the bike, given that a light, responsive, and speedy race bicycle costs anywhere from $2,000 to $10,000.

To win races (and move up through the categories), you need to accept the cycling adage that fast isn't healthy. Much like a pro, an amateur racer at his peak is forever on the verge of having a season's worth of dedication brought down by a sniffle, is always hungry, is eternally nursing spent muscles. The dedicated amateur feels spectacular when his specially trained body is on the bike flying past people, but breaks apart when he tries to do something normal, such as run across a yard to catch a Frisbee or lift a five-gallon bottle into a water cooler.

It's one thing to submit to endless hours of suffering and deprivation when you're riding for a paycheck, or for fame in the Tour de France; quite another when you have to go home after the race and mow the lawn.

I'd done five more warm-up laps since the Animal had left me, and I rolled once again over the painted white line that marked the start, sprint, and finish. Just off to the left of the 23-foot, 8-inch wide strip of asphalt was the tree under which two local race officials sat during the Crit, to ring a bell that announced the points lap, score the sprints, flip over numbers on a big counter that let us know what lap we were on, and to yank dropped riders out of the race.

I pedaled through the straight run of about 150 feet, which

lets the winners safely bleed off speed after a sprint, carved left with the first turn, then squiggled right and left before sweeping right for the lead-up to the Crit's only notable rise, a little hill that gains maybe twenty feet of elevation as it curves left. Little groups of red, yellow, blue, orange jerseys passed me. Most of them featured horrific color clashes and scrawls of words—the uniforms of amateur and pro teams bound to proclaim every sponsor they could find: Tru-Brew (the Animal's team), Colavita Olive Oil, Gotham Cyclists, Quark, Sun Valley, Tri-State Velo, Bike Line, BiKyle, Kutztown University, Navigators.

I was, in racing parlance, unattached. My plain red jersey said so.

Over the hill, at about the halfway point of the course, the pavement shoots down right, left and right, then into a lazy, leftward arc through a wooded section. As I pedaled through shadows, the course nearly imperceptibly rising again, tight little packs of three to five racers passed me, trailing a breeze spiced with faint whiffs of sweat, chain lube, the synthetic tang of energy gels, and the candied menthol aroma of liniment oil—called embrocation by cyclists and ritually spread on the legs before events. It smelled to me like spring, like speed, like points and dreams.

The arc of the course sharpened into a genuine left turn just as I exited the darkest part of the tree cover. Out of the corner and much, much farther away than it always looked—a heartbreaking distance—I could see the finish line.

There was a guy I knew standing up there, straddling his bike where the first row would eventually line up. As I pedaled past him, I slowed nearly to a standstill and, addressing him by his nickname, said, "Swerve, don't line up front row." The head of the pack was for cyclists with nicknames like the Animal, Speedy, Torch. There was a big 200-pounder called Scooter, who signified about the lowliest nickname that could legitimately start first or even second row.

I spun out another loop. Nobody talked to me. When I came around again, with about five minutes until race time, the field was lining up, spread across the pavement five or six wide, already ten rows deep. There would be eighty-three racers tonight. I pulled up beside Swerve, who'd retreated to the back. He was fitter than me and more than a decade younger, but for some reason I was always faster, which gave me the edge in the pecking order that exists in every on-bike acquaintanceship.

Swerve said, "I don't know what I was thinking." Then, right out loud, in a racing pack, where you could be judged feeble by the involuntary flicker of an eye, he said, "The truth is, I'm just not very confident about riding in a group."

I stared at him. He was on a new, sea-green Bianchi, an Italian bike brand with a storied lineage. Bianchis had won the Tour de France, the Tour of Italy, world championships, and had been used to set the most prestigious mark in cycling, the Hour Record. Marco Pantani, the troubled, brilliant champion who eventually committed suicide, but while healthy had nearly cracked Lance Armstrong in the mountains, had ridden a Bianchi. So had the greatest Italian racer of them all, Fausto Coppi. "Really, Bill," Swerve said, "do you think I'm ready for a pack this big?"

He was straw-thin, chiseled in the face, and had the kind of cycling legs so stripped down they appeared almost without muscle. If you knew what you were looking at, you could tell he was an insane mix of miles and disciplined eating. Out in public, walking along a sidewalk anywhere in the country, Swerve would look scrawny. Here in the Crit, you could see that he was carrying at least three unnecessary pounds on his upper body.

I thought of telling him I was in no position to pass judgment on him—that I couldn't even finish a race. Instead, I raised my handlebar half an inch, lifting the front wheel off the ground, and reached down with one hand and spun the wheel. It was what racers did when they were making sure their brakes weren't rubbing.

Colored helmets spread out in front of us, bobbing with their riders' movements like a field of some fantastic crop. The constant shifting of the single foot each rider had propped on the ground snapped out a metallic chorus, as if this strange field were populated by even stranger crickets.

"Are your brakes rubbing, Bill?" said Swerve.

I shook my head.

We waited for the start.

The pressure to confess to some weakness, a lack of training or nerve or proper gear, was like trying to hold back a cough. All around us, people strived to chat about the weather or anything else of no consequence.

"Bill. Hey, Bill. What do you think of Alaric?"

"He's dying, Swerve," I said. "The man is dying. That's what I think."

A whistle blew to start the race. I fumbled my foot around, trying to click into my pedal, and Swerve shot smoothly away, beginning the Thursday Night Crit far ahead of me.

* * *

About ten years earlier, Alaric Gayfer had been standing in the grassy infield of the velodrome when I showed up for the first day of an instructional program I'd signed up for—a kind of regular-people-give-these-funny-bikes-a-try introductory class. He was in his late thirties, already retired from pro racing, and into his second or third career as a coach. Under coarse yellow hair and a big-featured face, he carried a low center of gravity thanks to boulderlike glutes and thighs, so that he seemed much shorter than he was. He wore no special jacket, no whistle or clipboard or anything else that would identify him as the instructor, yet he was instantly recognizable as our leader.

There were maybe ten of us—some promising juniors, including a twelve- or thirteen-year-old girl with national-class and perhaps world-class talent, a couple of guys like me in their late twenties or early thirties, a retired racer trying to lose some weight (whom Alaric would quickly nickname Suds, which meant he could clean the track with us), and a few others scattered across ages and abilities and ambitions. We stood before him in a half circle.

"Awright," he said with his blokey British-American accent. "The rotten news I have to give you is that not all of you are going to turn into racers." His voice was not what could be accurately called loud; it was, instead, big. "No, sorry, then, I regret to inform you," he burred, filling the bowl of the football-field-size velodrome. "Not all of you can end up as racers. But any single one of you could be." He arched an eyebrow and stared at each of us in turn.

We began with the basics—learning to strap our feet into the pedals, getting used to how the non-coasting rear wheel would of its own momentum push the pedals around once you'd started it rolling, figuring out how to apply back-pressure to slow the bike. Then he coaxed us into whispering our front wheels up to within an inch of the rear wheel ahead of us, showed us how to safely dive down the steep banking of the velodrome, reminded us over and over to pull back on the handlebar instead of pushing down in a sprint, and to pass cyclists in one quick and decisive move—not, he said, as if we wanted to wrestle with them but as if we were stabbing them. Near the end of the summer, he began organizing us into little groups so we could try out the strategies and tactics real racers used.

While we spun around the velodrome, he'd stand in the infield, shuffling in circles to keep an eye on us while yelling instructions: "Suuuuuudddddds—nowwww!"

Out in turn four, Suds would know exactly what to do, springing off the thirteen-year-old girl's wheel to cross the finish five bike lengths clear, for a victory that embarrassed him and disappointed her. Alaric would begin walking toward the finish line then, giving one short wave of his hand to the girl. She would roll over to him. He'd grab her shoulder, lean in, and give quiet, wise advice. Next time she would finish only four bike lengths back.

Sometimes he would yell at me: "Biiiiilllllllll—"

But I could never tell if the second part of his command was "Goooo nooowwwww," or "Go dowwwwwwnnnn," or even "Not nowwwww!" So I'd pick something to do—abandon the sheltering draft of Suds's wheel and wrestle around him for 200 feet, so that at the line I could lose by four bike lengths to him and three bike lengths to the Princess of Genetics.

I'd take a recovery lap, rasping and blind. Still standing in the infield, Alaric would yell, "Biiiiiilllllll, wot 'appened?"

I'd replay the race in my head, then gasp something like, "I came around Suds on the far straight, but got caught by both of them." My voice would be barely audible; I almost could not hear myself. Even so, Alaric would scream, "Whyyyyy?"

I'd analyze the action as rigorously as I could. "Uh—I guess that—because I went too early to hold them off?"

Alaric would scream, "Whyyyyyyy?"

"Because maybe—I thought I was faster."

"Whyyyyyy?"

Everyone on the track, our class and the pro racers there to practice, could hear this.

"Because I thought—"

"Whyyyyyy?"

"I don't know, Alaric. I don't know."

I'd be back at the finish line. Alaric would give a short wave of his arm, and the future female champion would roll over to him. He'd grab her shoulder, lean in, and give his wise, quiet advice.

I was far from the best pupil in his class, and I was obviously not blessed with bike-racing genes. But I improved the most and, by the time the season was over, Alaric was visibly proud of what he'd done with me, a quality demonstrated with a jaunty lift of his right eyebrow and a sort of bemused look. We ended up becoming friends of a sort. Not good friends—we ran into each other maybe three or four times a year after that—but close friends, in the way that when we did see each other it felt as if the first one to speak was merely picking up the last conversational thread the other had left loose the last time we'd met.

For more than a year now, Alaric had been supposed to die of brain cancer, but had just kept on living, sometimes still riding his bike, once just a few days after brain surgery.

If he'd been at the Crit, Alaric would have yelled at me to forget about Swerve and find the Animal. For laps and laps now, I'd been pinned in the middle of the pack. The thrum of chains and the ratcheting of freewheels and guys yelling "Whoa!" or "Hey!" was loud and constant and everywhere, like riding in a train with the windows open. A blue-jerseyed shoulder rocked off me, leaned back onto me, and I laid myself full against it. To my right, an elbow flicked mine. I drew my arm in to absorb the contact, leaning hard for counterbalance against the blue shoulder. A rear wheel nicked my front wheel and I leaned into that—if I snapped my wheel away in panic, I'd spiral into a series of accelerating wobbles and eventually crash. I could sit in here until I popped again, like I'd done every week so far, or I could at least try something. I could *goooooo nooooooow*.

I jabbed my elbow against Blue Jersey and drove my bike left, drilling open a gap. I squirmed out of the pack, giving up its shelter. Alone in the wind, I burned most of the energy left in my body passing six or seven rows of riders. When I got to the second row, I heeled my bike right, stuck my wheel in a tiny sliver between bicycles, and moved someone backward. I was in.

The Animal was one row ahead of me, in the front and three or four riders to my right. We came up onto the hill and stood up out of our saddles and ran on our pedals.

A tiny woman in an orange-and-blue jersey, a pro from somewhere in South America who had a butt shaped like a garlic clove, jammed into me from the right, trying to bump me off the Animal's wheel. All of the best male racers here could be legitimately called national- or world-class, but even within that elite slice of the sport there were gradations. Less than a handful could say they were or once had been good enough to ride alongside the sport's greatest champions. A few more were gifted and gritty enough to have made it, or be assured of at least a shot at making it, to the exalted pro level in Europe. Many more could be considered among the finest pro or amateur racers in the United States. For sure, though, any woman who could consistently ride at the front of this pack was a rare and amazing athlete, deserving of a champion's respect. But I wasn't going to relinquish the Animal's wheel, so I piled my Cat 5 shoulder against Clove and held my spot.

We slung around the course like mad dogs at the end of a staked chain, and when we crossed the line and the bell clanged to announce a points lap, the Animal made his move.

He didn't really attack. It was more like he'd just gone slightly faster than the group and inadvertently gotten a gap. It was so subtle I almost didn't follow him, thinking I should wait for him to notice his mistake and fade back. But I held his wheel just to make sure Clove didn't get it, and the two of us crept out in front of the wall of the pack. We had a gap of ten feet. Then fifteen, then two riders jumped across the open

23

space and there were four of us. One of them exploded immediately from the effort of bridging.

Points went four deep, and there were three of us. All I had
to do was hang for one mile.

The Animal looked back, and did this thing where he scooted
to the rear of his seat and stretched his legs as he pedaled. Our
speed ticked up another two digits, into the mid-thirties. He was
widening the gap, riding away from a pack of eighty racers. We
went over the hill and down, and he threw another mph into his
bike, and it was then that I knew I couldn't stay on his wheel.
Even with him in front, shielding me from the wind, burning
himself up while I hid, my body was shutting itself down.

I couldn't hang.

I had to.

I might die if I did.

I cursed Swerve for putting the thought of mortality into
my head.

We really could die out there. Despite the routine occurrence of
broken wrists, smashed collarbones, and flayed skin among
amateur racers, cycling is not what most of the general public
would think of as a risky sport. Downhill skiing, half-pipe
snowboarding, base jumping, motorcycle racing—those were
sports that could go spectacularly bad. Cycling is not dangerous in that way, but with surprising frequency it can be deadly.

A few years earlier, a beautiful, eternally cheery twenty-four-
year-old rising star who'd trained on the same roads I often did,
Nicole Reinhart, had hit a tree during a race, and died. At least
a few times a year, a pro cyclist would plummet off a high cliff
in Europe. In a race across America a guy had gotten creamed

by a truck. And there were always cardiac arrests: The combination of heat, dehydration, and cardiovascular systems working at their max regularly felled pro and amateur cyclists. For years, I'd known that I was probably going to die on a bike.

My father had been killed by a heart attack at forty-seven; his brother at fifty-six. A cardiologist had told me that, probably like them, I had a genetic predisposition for heart disease—I was four times more likely to die of it than the average guy. If I rode aerobically, at a casual pace no harder than 60–70 percent of my maximum, the doctor had explained, cycling was so beneficial to my body that, over time, my general risk might drop by half. But, he continued, any time I rode all-out, the chance of sudden cardiac death would jump, perhaps as much as seven-fold.

While it was technically true that there were hundreds of moments in every Crit when I was twenty-eight times more likely to die than if I were sitting on a couch, ordinarily that stat felt as relevant to me as the one about driving to work being more dangerous than skydiving. But, there on the Animal's wheel, my brain began discussing the situation, like a ship's captain giving a droll lecture to visitors while a catastrophe down in the steam room was scalding the crew. Would I rather score a point or would I rather back off, get dropped again, yet be assured that after the race I would drive home and romp around the yard that night with Beth and Natalie? One point isn't worth not getting to do that, was my head's first opinion. Yet, it countered, if Alaric, who really was dying, could be here racing right now, wouldn't he say that living was not worth never trying to score a point?

Especially if he knew what ten points was all about.

* * *

I held the wheel. My entire cognitive digression had passed the time for another 50 feet or so of asphalt, and we were at the last corner. I breathed like a man with dry heaves. My leg muscles began to go off like strings of firecrackers, little pops of pain starting down at my feet and working their way up until my quads were scorched confetti.

I held the wheel.

I snuck a peek back, under my shoulder in the gap between my arm and chest. We'd dropped the third rider, who dangled like a miserable speck between us and an onrushing wall of color. If we held this speed, the Animal and I would cross the line just in front of the pack.

I was holding the Animal's wheel. I was not getting dropped. I was going to score. Then I was tumbling down into my own body, gasping and choking and trying to stick my head up above my exhaustion to snatch a breath as ten bikes or more streamed past me, lined out, sprinted, scored points, and regrouped.

The rest of the pack dopplered past, receded in front of me, then dived below a far horizon of asphalt. Swerve, Blue Jersey, Clove, all in there somewhere. Next came the stragglers we'd busted off earlier. They split around me as they passed, reforming into a slow, senseless chase that would never catch sight of the pack, let alone actually catch it.

Whatever the real odds had been, I'd been willing to ride so hard I died, and it wasn't enough.

I rode into the woods alone, then quit. The Animal scored 29 points that night.

four

"DOES IT HURT?" ASKED NATALIE.

"Yes," I told her.

"A lot?"

"I don't know."

Our German shepherd, Tigger, was stretched out between us on the floor of the utility room. Her snout lay in Natalie's lap. Her back legs, which were stretched over my lap, kept making those twitches that dogs fire off when someone touches their slim hind bones. Tig was more than a hundred pounds, but her legs felt so fragile. I understood the twitches. I patted her stomach and said, "She trusts you a lot, Nat."

"I know," said my daughter as she ran her tiny palm along the short brown hairs of the six-year-old shepherd's nose. Tigger expelled an enormous amount of air from her lungs and rolled her head in quarter-turns from side to side. She whined, just a little.

Without grasping her lower leg, I touched the wound on the meatiest part of her left haunch. She didn't jerk this time.

"Oh, Tiggy, Tiggy, Tiggy," cooed Nat. At five, she was better with animals than I was with anything in life. Tigger whimpered, then seemed to fall asleep.

I figured that she'd been nicked by a ricocheting piece of buckshot. Pennsylvania is a hunter's state—opening day of deer season is an excused absence at many schools—and even out of season, poachers roamed the edges of my family's four-acre woods. Tigger mostly lay on our porch and watched the deer pass through the brush or graze in Beth's gardens. She'd long since learned she could never catch even the youngest doe, but sometimes a mood of doggy optimism would take her and she'd gallop into the woods. For all her size, though, if she ever caught a deer, she'd be more likely to fetch it back to us rather than kill it.

Our mongrel cat, Jasper, was the predator: mice, moles, voles, grackles, frogs, toads, ducks, baby geese. One morning I opened the front door to find him standing just beyond the porch, meowing over a deer's foreleg he'd dragged up for display. Natalie became convinced Jasper had felled a buck, a feat that made her equally sad and proud.

Jasper's nickname after that: Mighty Hunter. I thought of Mighty an inordinate amount when I rode. It was life or death for him out there in our woods every single night. The real deal. The cosmic struggle on the primal level. When he meowed to be let out, he risked the teeth of the fox for the taste of the mouse. I needed some of that—which I had been explaining to my friend Jeremy as we rode in the morning before Tigger got shot.

"So," Jeremy said, "your cycling inspiration is a house cat?"

"Half house cat," I amended. We were climbing a hill called Acorn, up out of the valley behind my mountain, which we'd already passed over. We climbed to stay warm, yet because we were purposely riding slowly—talking all the time to make sure we kept our heart rates down—we couldn't quite pedal the chatter out of our voices.

I'd gotten up at 4:50 A.M., rising to the first soft beep of the alarm on my heart-rate monitor, which I'd taken to wearing as a wristwatch—so it could wake me in the mornings and so I'd have one less piece of gear to fuss with in the dark. Sunrise rides were the only way I'd ever get the right kind of miles. At the lunch rides, with a feisty pack of locals and colleagues who wanted to blow off workday stress, I was too often lured into sprints and contests for the hilltops. It was the long, lazy, day-eating rides that let muscles heal, coaxed the body into sprouting new capillaries, spun waste out of the legs, and hastened recovery even more than a day off the bike would. Passing time on a casual ride once, a racer named Rocket told me that the faster you are, the slower you can go. It's the vain, recreational riders who fancy themselves fast—one of which I used to be—who throw themselves through every ride at their mediocre top speeds.

In March I'd begun to supplement my daily lunch-ride schedule by getting out onto the road by 5 A.M. That way I could ease away two hours and still get home in time to fix Natalie breakfast, or sometimes catch her and Beth still snuggled in our bed, where Natalie came each morning after waking. Beth would almost never be asleep at that hour, but she liked to lie there after she woke up and hold Natalie—smell her hair, touch the big freckle under her ear, watch her chest rise and fall, and try to divine her dreams from the flickering of her closed eyes.

A few mornings, both of them had been sleeping in. Beth's hair, lying across Nat's on the pillow they shared, was browner and coarser than our daughter's, but indisputably spun from the same genetic weave. Beth's face, too, had unmistakably lent its contours to Nat, but was more intricate; instead of the round freshness of our daughter's features, Beth possessed forty years' worth of life's etchings and carvings. There were wrinkles just starting to burrow out from the edges of her mouth. There was a droop coming to the tip of her nose that you would notice only if, like me, you'd fallen in love with the tilt of that nose nearly two decades earlier. I stood beside the bed for more than ten minutes once, studying her until she awoke, and I was startled to see that even in her first second of consciousness there was a weathered sensibility about her eyes that deepened their beauty, the way a nimbus sky can be more striking than a clear blue day.

Jeremy and I crested Acorn and spun our pedals up from a climbing cadence of 60 rpm to 100. We slapped our fingers against the shifters nested on the brake levers, dropping our chains onto harder gears, and began to spin those out as we descended into another valley. Our breath puffed out in front of us and we rode through it, over and over and over. We passed a farm named Stone Pony and spent fifteen minutes imagining tales of its origin. We talked about Jeremy's new jacket. We talked about Steak, who would never get up early enough to ride with us. I told a story about the one morning I'd cajoled him out, when he'd said, "The thing is, I could be lying next to a warm, naked woman right now," and how contemplating his priorities nearly made me absolve him. Somewhere in there I rode my two thousandth mile of the year, an event I didn't notice until I flipped to my odometer to pass some more time and saw that it read 2008, and for twenty minutes we talked about how mileage doesn't really matter, yet it's the thing cyclists most often lie about. Weak riders brag high, strong riders sandbag low. And we talked about all the weak and strong riders we knew, and all the time we talked I could only think of one thing.

I had no points.

We rode onto a street where some enormous, pink-flowered tree had bloomed fatally early and was losing all of its petals in a brilliant death, laying down a carpet of cotton-candy warmth over the pavement, stunning in beauty and tragedy. And all I could think of it was: This is how the world will look when I score points.

I didn't talk about that.

When I rode into our drive, Natalie ran out to meet me and shouted, "Dadda! Tigger got bit."

But when I got in the house and Beth and Natalie and I examined Tigger, I could see she hadn't been bit. She'd been shot. I knew what that looked like.

"Between his eyes or in his ass?" my father asked, aiming the gun at Prince, and even back then, at age eight, I knew by long experience that saying "I don't know" meant my father would inflict both choices: make me pay for something I'd damaged, for instance, and also take away my allowance for the next two weeks; put one toy in the closet for a week and smash the other with his foot. So I didn't hesitate, not even a second. I said, "Shoot him in the butt."

* * *

Before Beth left for work, she brought out the plastic bin in which she'd organized our medical supplies. We have a natural division of labor. She schedules and maintains, and buys the plastic boxes and the things in them that I need to clean up the spectacular disasters. I deal with ticks, vomit, poop, pee, blood, garbage, busted pipes, dirty bikes, broken taillights, fallen trees, and hole digging. I'd craved Beth physically the second I saw her, but it was plastic boxes of supplies that had kept us together for almost twenty years.

"We don't need a veterinarian?" Natalie asked.

"How do you know that word?" I said.

Beth set hydrogen peroxide, tweezers, scissors, gauze, and a tube of Neosporin on the floor of the utility room. "Don't worry," she said to Nat. "If your dad says he can handle this, you know he can. Besides, Tigger would rather have us take care of her, right?"

Natalie nodded. She didn't question how I knew how to take care of bullet wounds. It was, to her, the same as me knowing how to make a peanut butter sandwich. Beth reached out and combed through Natalie's hair with her fingers. With her hand still tickling the base of Nat's neck, Beth bent at the waist and leaned toward me for a kiss good-bye. Our lips brushed, then she surprised me by flicking the tip of her tongue against my lips, light and quick. She pulled back and said, "You're a great dad. Love you guys," and left.

Nat said, "The peroxide stings?"

"Yeah."

She stroked Tigger, leaning down to peer into the dog's eyes then kissing her on the forehead even though Tigger smelled like a swamp from playing in the muddy pond behind our house.

"Okay," I said, "here we go." I poured the hydrogen peroxide onto a rag.

"Daddy," said Nat.

"What?" I asked.

"You are a great daddy. You're a great daddy to our doggy, Daddy."

I dabbed at Tigger's wound. The edges were sharp and clean on both sides. The hole oozed bright red blood and clear fluid without spilling out any fat, or bone, or loose tendons or tissue, and I could see the dull, hard surface of the single piece of shot lodged in there.

After school one day, I'd gone out to feed my collie-and-shepherd mix. We kept him chained to a tree in our backyard, and I had this game with him. I'd kneel down and cradle his head between mine and my shoulder, and take the chain and slide it back and forth beneath him, and he'd skip his feet over it without being able to see it, dancing, light and quick, showing off. I'd stop and he'd cover my face with licks. I was fascinated by the speed of instinct. We played our game. He licked my face.

He was quick, so quick on his feet. I was proud of him. I emptied a metal cup of Purina into his dented bowl.

When I went back into the house, and walked up the three steps from the door to the landing and then through the kitchen into the dining room, where a double-wide sliding-glass door looked out on the backyard, my father was waiting there. He was big to me then, about five foot eight or five foot nine, and he was in his thirties and had a complete but sparse covering of brown hair, wore silver glasses. He was thin, always thin, and had a slash of mouth across a square chin— mostly my face, I guess. He said, "What was that?"

His irises seemed to bounce around the insides of his eyeballs.

"Game," I said. I started to swallow, then stopped the motion halfway and held the sensation hard in my throat. The best thing was not to move at all. I tried to breathe without moving my chest. My heart sounded like a sledgehammer hitting wood.

I watched the dark holes of my father's eyes rattle around. With the deliberation of an hour hand, I tucked my chin into my chest.

"I'll show you," said my father, "a game that'll cripple a goddamn dog."

He left the room. I waited for him to come back. My sister, Leann, who was three, peeked her head around the wall where the dining room opened onto the living room. I shook my head at her and she disappeared. There was a big, tan chair in a corner that she liked to hide behind.

He was carrying a shotgun when he came back, thrown upside down over his right shoulder as if he was on a Confederate march, index finger of his right hand hooked through the trigger guard. When he got within a couple steps of me, he flipped the barrel forward off his shoulder and somehow in one sliding motion linked two distinct mechanical operations that, by their sound, told you the gun was cocked. He stood there ready to fire from the hip.

"Open the door," he said.

My father was a great shot. A friend and I had once been sitting on the concrete patio steps outside the sliding door, shooting a BB gun at a pair of empty beer cans on the cement-block steps about halfway across the yard. My father had flung open the door, gestured for our toy, taken it, and, holding it aloft only with the hand that squeezed the trigger, fired off a single shot that knocked both cans down. I'd also seen him pick running rats off junked cars, take the heads off squirrels, win beer after beer after beer knocking sparrows out of the air with his friends.

I turned my back on my father. I walked to the door and clicked the lock and slid the heavy glass panel back on its track. Prince stood and looked at me. He raised his ears.

Behind me, my father said, "You choose. Between his eyes or in his ass?"

"Butt," I said instantly. "It was a game. Don't kill him."

The dining room floor creaked. Closer to me now, he said, "You might as well kill a dog as cripple it."

"I said butt."

The floor creaked. I could smell the oil of the muzzle just behind me. Prince wagged his tail, stretched low on his front paws, beckoning me. From the living room, I could hear Leann, not crying, not shouting, pleading somehow without words.

"Butt," said my father, low, "was not a choice. It was eyes or ass. You blew it."

Leann's voice became a high keen. I turned and saw the shotgun just off my cheek and I said, "Please. Please, Dad."

"Please what?"

"Please shoot Prince in the ass."

He shoved me sideways away from the gun and squeezed the trigger.

The dog yelped, and Natalie soothed its head back down, saying, "Oh, Tiggy Tiggy Tiggy."

I put the tiny, bloody piece of shot I'd tweezed out of Tigger onto a folded paper towel and showed it to Nat. I snipped away hair, clearing an egg-sized spot of open, flaky white skin, then clipped off a few bits of ragged tissue around the wound. Tigger squirmed. I probed into the hole with my little finger to make sure there was no debris left in her body, then smeared Neosporin on my index finger and swabbed the wound and the circle of pale skin.

Natalie kissed Tigger's nose.

I had said, "You choose," to Natalie one day.

She believed that her stuffed kittens—all eighty-three of which she'd given not only names but distinct personalities, family histories, and extensive backgrounds—were what she called "real." She lived in a world in which she understood that her toy cats were not alive like her pets, but was equally convinced that they contained some expressive essence called realness that existed between the inanimate and the breathing.

Beth and I had discovered that our most effective disciplinary action—better than time-outs or a cartoon ban—was to take one of Nat's kittens away for a night. As her tolerance grew, we took more than one kitten, for more than one night. Once, when Natalie had colored on a wall during a playdate, I'd banished every kitten to my closet for a week.

A few months ago, I'd threatened to exercise the pandemic option again.

"I don't care," said Nat. "I get them back."

"Fine," I said. "Two weeks."

"They go on vacation," Natalie said. "They come back happy. Go ahead and take them."

Beth and Natalie and I were in the hallway between her bedroom and ours. I pushed past her, into her room, came back with a random armful of cats I'd swiped off her bed, and scattered them onto the king-size bed where Beth and I slept. One of Natalie's living cats, Milo, a gray-and-white stray, leaped off the bed and scampered out the door.

"You pick one," I said, breathing hard. "And I'm throwing that one away."

"Bill," said Beth.

"Pick one," I shouted. "In the trash. To get burned."

Natalie's chin quivered, steadied, broke again, and her mouth opened. No sound came out. Her eyes shined.

"You choose," I said, "or they all get burned." I swept my arms back across the toys, except they were not toys. They were real.

"That's enough," Beth said. "This is going way too far, Bill." She stepped forward and dropped a hand on Natalie's shoulder, and said, "Nothing's getting burned," and started to kneel down beside her. But Natalie ducked under the hand and took a step toward the bed and loosed a torrent of tears and snot and, trembling everywhere—arms, fingers, knees, head—made her way to the bed and picked up an orange kitten and said, "Good-bye, Thomas, I loved you," and kissed its nose and handed it to me. And looked into my eyes.

* * *

I swallowed, and patted Tig's haunch. "She's okay," I said.

Prince had been okay, too, taking just a couple of pellets in the haunch. My father was a great shot, but Prince was light, pure light on his feet. And Thomas the kitten had survived. I'd put him on a high shelf in the kitchen, telling Beth as I hid him in there, "I know you were right. I was going to stop after you said that. But then I felt like she called my bluff or something." Beth hadn't said anything. I'd said, "I'm going to give him back in a few hours." Beth still hadn't said anything. "And apologize," I'd said, and Beth had nodded.

By the time Natalie convinced me to pour some of her liquid children's Motrin over a slice of deli turkey and feed it to Tigger, it was way after nine o'clock. I was late for work, and she was late for preschool. But since we were already late, she reasoned, why couldn't she have five more minutes to draw a get-well card? Then she had to tape the card to the wall by Tigger's bed. We weren't out on the driveway, striding toward our ratty pickup, until nearly 9:30. A few steps from the truck, I noticed that Natalie had forgotten her jacket.

"Dammit," I said. "Stay here." I rushed back into the house, grabbed Natalie's jacket, and blew back out through the door. I threw the jacket at her as I passed, and it draped over her face and shoulders.

Natalie said, "Daddy! Stop!" She flailed her arms under the jacket and tore it off her head.

"We're late," I growled. "We're going." I loped around the truck to unlock her door.

"This is important." She was trilling up behind me, skipping to match my long steps. "Can we stop? Please? Please, Daddy?"

I halted. I flipped my arm and looked at my watch, more a gesture of my anger than an actual search for information. "Goddammit, Natalie," I said, "what is it now?"

She was breathing fast. "Listen, Daddy. Guess what I forgot?"

I started walking back toward the garage. "What?"

"Daddy. Listen."

I stopped, turned, and looked at her. She dropped her jacket from her hands and squatted down on the driveway. She said, "I forgot that I'm not a frog," and she began hopping toward me.

I shook my head.

"Now," she said, "I forget that I'm not a kitty," and she sat back on her haunches and meowed.

I tried to keep the smile from crinkling across my mouth.

"Daddy. What do you forget?"

"I forget . . ." I paused.

"Raaaar—hisss!" She'd pounced at me, and she stuck out her claw and scratched at my calf. "I forget I'm not a mad cat! What do you forget, Daddy? What?"

My daughter clawed at me, and hissed and roared.

I said, "When I'm with you, beautiful girl, I forget that I can't score ten points." Sometimes I could even forget why I needed to.

five

I WAS WHITE TRASH. I USED THE PHRASE TO DESCRIBE myself the way other people say "I'm Irish," or "I'm Jewish." It was my heritage. It was my blood. We were not crackers or hillbillies or Yanks or Pilgrims or Appalachians or Midwesterners. No matter where my family scattered, or how high our incomes climbed, we were white trash.

We were always, however, the finest grade of rubbish. By and large, through the generations as long as any of us could remember, our veins had coursed with charisma, smarts, and strength that put us atop the heap of our people, yet were linked to a primal urge for self-destruction that prevented us from ever actually rising away.

There was a cousin my age, a swift and fearless athlete who would fling himself happily into either a footrace or a fistfight with not just anyone but any number of opponents—once facing down three late-teen badasses when we were just in the sixth grade—and who, because he was biracial, was knifed and killed in his twenties in a hate crime carried out as revenge for a theft he'd been involved in. There was a female relative and her mother, both gifted with a careless gutter beauty, who decayed into bonafide crack whores. There was my pool-hustler uncle, who could run tables clear of balls from the time the bars opened until they closed, run them when he was so drunk he could not stand without leaning against the pool cue; and he was so charming while taking people's money that they ended up calling him their friend. He hung himself in jail.

There was my father, Billy Joe Strickland. He was born amid the coal holes and chemical valleys of West Virginia— the raped-and-razed part John Denver never sang about. Family lore has it that the drunk doctor who delivered him, right there in what my grandmother always described as "the sitting room" of her house, thought "William Joseph" aimed too high for the child he'd seen, and wrote "Billy Joe" on the birth certificate. My father told me, just once, that his father, Bill, had threatened to kill the doctor if his son was christened with such a name as "William." That Bill, a coal miner, a man whom I never knew because he died of cancer or black lung before I was born, and because my father told me no stories about him, looked to me in the few cracking black-and-white photos I had of him to be the hardest of all the family.

My grandmother once told me that when my father was a kid, getting straight As and still being happy to fight any boy on the playground came to him as easily as breathing—but that he'd never be able to get Bs and not fight. Most of his school pictures showed him with bruises, cuts on the side of his mouth, mussed hair.

He tried to escape our ancestral curse, joining the Air Force to get out of his hometown, carousing through Germany in sharp suits and black-rimmed glasses and convertibles, making friends who smiled and flipped the good-natured bird at the camera in all their pictures, ending up in his twenties in Gary, Indiana, where the steel mills and their strong unions promised a middle-class life—a miracle for a white-trash scrapper promised only an inheritance of annihilation. He'd gone farther and climbed higher than anyone in his family ever had.

He worked at the blast furnaces, the thirty-story infernos in which they melt iron ore into molten metal, and he met my mother, Frances James. Everyone had called her Cookie since infancy when her aunt asked one day, "How's our little cookie doing?" Her mother was the kind of wage-earning dancer that in those days was called a go-go girl. (Later, when I was three or four and would sometimes eat lunch at the Coconut Grove, where my grandmother worked, I picked up on her stage name and for years called her Hot Pants.) Her father, who had confessed to the delivery team at the hospital that he was afraid his daughter's face would be scarred from his syphilis, never really became part of her family and left for good when, at a crowded Thanksgiving dinner table, four-year-old Cookie announced that she didn't like her dad because "he hits my mommy and makes her sad." After even that semblance of a home came apart, my mother and her siblings were adopted and raised by their grandparents. My mother's sister would one day go to the county fair and never come home, having run off for a life as a carnie. My mother must have instantly understood my father's flight from destruction. She, too, wanted to be normal.

For her, it wasn't a matter of locking away something awful

within herself, but of walling off as much of the madness around her as she could and within that channel laying down her will like a set of railroad tracks. My mother's determination and stubbornness was legendary within our family. After one argument of never-explained provenance with her grandfather, she didn't speak to him for four years. While carrying me one winter day, she slipped on some icy stairs and, cradling me to the safety of her chest with both arms rather than trying to break her fall, ended up in the hospital with a back that would bother her for the rest of her life.

Once, my father and some of his friends had decided to overhaul an engine, dropped part of it on the garage floor behind my mother's car, then started drinking and lost all interest in the field of automobile repair.

"You gotta move it," my mother said the next morning. "I have to get to work."

"Cook, that thing isn't going anywhere," my father said. "It must weigh three hundred pounds."

My mother was barely five feet tall, a big sixties sculpture of black hair cascading around round cheeks and a prominent nose. She was almost sinewy in her slenderness—the most athletic-looking of our family, including the person I turned out to be. In her teens she'd been a featured dancer on *American Bandstand*, and at some point before marrying had performed in some never fully explained capacity as a trapeze artist. She dropped her purse to the garage floor and, in a short black dress split vertically by a line of silver, walked over to the engine, squatted, positioned her upturned forearms under two protruding metal pieces, lifted the thing a few inches off the ground, and crabbed it over into a corner.

My father bragged about that feat the rest of his life. "If you get in Cookie's way, she'll move you or flatten you," he'd conclude the story. It was genuine admiration, but probably also a reminder to himself.

By the time I was born, my father had become an alcoholic and a drug addict—and a salesman. An industrial accident at the steel mill had spewed carbon monoxide into his plant, sending him into a coma from which he was never supposed to emerge. He recovered, but suffered forever after from grand mal epileptic seizures—the big violent ones with full-body thrashing, spitting, choking. He was no longer fit to work at the steel mill, but with his penchant for spinning failure into good fortune, he found his true calling. He sold, throughout his life, print advertising, radio time, real estate, insurance, Better Business Bureau memberships, lawn-care programs, used cars, shoes, cigarettes, family portraits, and time shares.

One morning before an interview he'd set up for a new job, I came down the steps from my bedroom just as the sun rose and there was my father, already awake and preparing for his day. He was on his hands and knees in the living room, wearing nothing but black dress socks and white briefs that were ripped at the waistband. A clear bottle with a red and blue label lay fallen on the floor, on its side, lid off, next to a big, orange, hand-blown glass ashtray we'd gotten as a souvenir on a vacation back to West Virginia a few years earlier. My father shivered and jerked. He dropped from his hands to his elbows, lowered his head to the ashtray, and lapped up the vodka in it. I'd seen this before. When he was unable to hold the bottle steady enough to get it to his mouth, he'd spill enough booze into the ashtray to help him overcome the shakes. I walked over to my father, and I put my hand on his back.

I petted him.

The first time I'd seen this house we lived in, he'd been selling real estate. On a Saturday afternoon he piled all of us—my mother, my sister, and me—into the car for a drive. This was a ritual. If my sister and I spotted a house with a For Sale sign my father didn't already know about, we'd get to stop at Dairy Queen. And if he went on to sell the house, we'd get fifty bucks.

"There's one!" I shouted, spying a For Sale by Owner sign on a big corner lot at the bottom of a hill in East Gary, a safer, less-poor suburb of the mill town. It was not quite like the neighborhoods we saw on sitcoms, but it was, at least, the kind of place where foremen lived, or those laborers who didn't squander paychecks or find themselves pawning jewelry as a regular source of family income. The house was big, two stories, white, with a haphazard mini-forest of oaks and a one-car garage. Farther down on the block, some kids played on green lawns and dogs ran up and down the sidewalks.

My father said, "Too late, Billy. Somebody already bought it."

I looked at the sign again. "There's no 'sold' sticker."

A pause. My father had stopped the car in the road beside the house and he looked at each of us in turn, wanting, I think, to preserve this moment when he alone could accurately see the outline of our future. He pulled into the driveway. He turned to my mother.

"Why don't you put the sticker on," he said to her, pulling one up from under his seat. "It's ours."

I scampered out of the car with Leann, who at five years

younger than me was two, and we swooped across and down the slope of the yard with our arms spread like wings. I felt rich and weightless, and free and warm in the summer sun of our new home. When my sister and I returned to the car, my father and mother were looking up at the house as he talked about the unfinished attic and how it would eventually become my bedroom, and how we would fence off the backyard for a dog we would get. My mother was looking not at the parts of the house my father gestured to, nor at his dancing hands, but directly up into his face, watching his mouth form these tales of our lives to come, watching his eyes reflect these visions. She reached up, put two fingers on his chin, and guided his face down to her and kissed him.

"So you accept my apology," he said.

He'd bought the house as a surprise, to make up for some argument. (Large-scale affections and hostilities were not new to us. The tiny, flat-roofed, clapboard house we were moving from had been painted completely orange by my mother one day when my father was at work, in retaliation for some other fight.)

Homes, cars, a moped, an anniversary cruise, a trip to Europe. Then food stamps, repossessed vehicles, a Christmas where the only presents were those a family friend brought by the day before, pants so short even our poorest friends could ridicule us, frigid winter nights when we had no oil for the furnace. As my father fought his destiny, our fortunes rose and fell in rolling waves of prosperity and poverty, neither state ever worth your despair or joy because you always knew the next would crash over you soon. At one point my mother tried taking jobs that might provide us with some small measure of stability—secretary at a screw-and-bolt manufacturer, assistant manager of a bowling alley. My father insulted her bosses, got her fired by stealing bowling pins to burn when we ran out of oil, and used her earnings to begin a career of tax evasion that would haunt my mother for years after his death. He set one of our cars on fire to collect the insurance. In the same week my mother's car got repossessed, he burned up another car, his old Granada, because it needed a repair he thought was too expensive. He watched the flaming engine until the firemen put it out, then hitched a ride with one of them he knew. A few hours later he drove up in a new sports car.

He could talk to anyone, which is why he could sell. His ill-fitting suits over shirts with collars not meant to be worn under jackets, cheap pens, and flashes of high-school-education diction all marked him clearly as white trash. Yet he owned a priceless, natural feel for reaching across the divide to engage successful people of a certain type—those who felt they'd had to hardscrabble their way up and saw something nostalgic in my father. He could just as easily commune with those who, like him, felt they'd been cheated by life, that the grand scope of their existence hadn't been recognized. The crushingly flat poor, he could elevate beyond their own starved dreams as he talked. The sad, those with chips on their shoulders, the lonely, the horny, the cautious, the silly, the scared—my father could find the one thing in anyone that he could connect with, an emotion he mirrored somewhere in himself. It wasn't so much that he had charisma, but he magnified—or invented—charisma in the person he focused on. He made everyone feel important, better, stronger, more generous, more proud of what they'd accomplished; he made them see their lives as an epic that was central to it all, rather than some ordinary struggle simply to do the same things today they'd done yesterday. You'd met someone who understood that you mattered.

Everything made sense in the presence of my father. Anything made sense.

On a summer day when I was between first and second grade, my father decided I was faster than the curly terror of our block—a neighbor's poodle. The tiny white fiend was unloved, unkempt, had no cute pom-poms on its tail, and, when driven from its house, roamed the sidewalks frothy with unfulfillable vengeance. It had nipped and bitten kids who lived all around us, free to stalk the neighborhood in that era when things like dog bites and fistfights between kids, and even adults, were settled among those who lived there.

My dad was arguing with the neighbor, yelling at the wide, heavy man in a white tank top that strained to hold in a belly that looked as if he swallowed poodles for dinner each night. He was just as loud as my dad, but their argument had a levity to it, a sense that each man was aware of being a performer in a winking show of exaggerated braggadocio. It was barely summer, the grass still blasting its newborn greenness onto the neighborhood's palette and its fragrance still one of birth rather than endurance. The sky was the blue you might color when you started back to school and had to depict your summer vacation.

Some kind of bet was being arranged. The poodle and I stood by with slightly bored expressions on our faces, as if we were grizzled prizefighters watching our managers hype a match. This was my father at his finest, not only organizing some caper no one else ever could have thought of, but imbuing the whole thing with layers of meaning that were fully clear only to him. Racing a poodle was ridiculous, yet would decide something of import. He boasted that he and I would vanquish the dog, yet my memory of the race is suffused with the impression that he also promised to redeem the poodle's reputation, and to restore the pride and innocent love of pet ownership to the neighbor. He rhapsodized and bullied and posited and appealed until he found the one opening that would entice the neighbor into the world he was describing, a place of significance, where ideals such as right and wrong were at that very moment ripe to be decided by us.

The dog was a dirty, streaky, dull pearl color, except for its teeth, which flashed white. Its gums, and the serrated tissue at the edge of its lips, were the blackest things you could see outside on that summer day. I remembered a story my dad had once told me about a midget he'd seen whip three guys in a bar fight, ending the anecdote with this advice: "Never get something small angrier than it is big."

The neighbor boomed, "But only if the boy gets a head start." He had stubble on his face and thin hair scraped across his head. He was barefoot, like me, and holding a sweaty beer can, like my father. He squatted and set the can in the grass. He grabbed his poodle by the scruff on either side of its neck and shook it back and forth. "Your boy'll never outrun her otherwise."

"Bullshit," said my dad. "We don't need a head start. Billy, do you need a head start?"

I looked at the poodle, which through the sheer internal heat of its bloodlust was spouting steam from its muzzle. I'd witnessed that miniature menace chasing down other kids—older kids, like the two brothers next door who were so mature they decorated their shared room with blacklight posters. The poodle had taken kids down on lawns, on sidewalks, in the road, going over fences.

"No, Dad," I said. "I don't need a head start."

"My boy don't need a head start," my dad proclaimed, as if I'd burst into a courtroom with a shocking piece of evidence for his side.

It was determined that the dog and I would race all the way across our yard and onto the driveway, which was the finish line. My father instructed me that when I reached the pavement, I was to cut sharply right and leap onto the trunk of our car, because neither adult would be at the finish to fend off the poodle. The neighbor had to stay back to hold and release the dog, and my father said he needed to be on the line to make sure there wasn't a mis-start.

"Ready?" asked my dad. "This is for all the goddamn marbles, now. Go!"

I sprang away. The neighbor gave me a generous step and a half, a head start that was significant yet not so blatant that my father would negate the race. I flung my leg forward again, then got a full stride, and with the next foot was at a run. Just as I took the next step, my bare right foot squashed a bee.

It stung me as it died. I took another step and one more before I could react, then I stopped, and hopped on one foot while I cradled the other in my hands, bent up at the knee, looking for the spot that burned. The poodle plowed into me and bit me on the calf of my left leg.

After the ice cube grew too cold against my skin, and the

two punctures no longer bled, and I demonstrated for my neighbor that I could walk, my dad carried me around the yard, holding me against his shoulder. His white T-shirt grew gray and wet with my tears. He patted me on the back and stroked my hair, as I have patted and stroked Natalie.

"Damn, Billy boy," he said. "You had him."

I sniffled. I nodded against his shoulder, smearing my nose across his shirt.

"I really think you would have outrun him," my dad said. "I'm counting that as a win. That goes in the books as a victory. Imagine that. Billy Strickland is fleeter than a goddamn dog."

"Yeah," I said.

"Well," said my dad, "we learned something important, to-day, right? You can't outrun a poodle if you step on a honey-bee."

I was weak as a child. I cried too easily, more often and with less provocation than was right for a Strickland. To make sure I understood this failing, from as far back as I can remember, I was not Billy, or Bill Junior, or even Little Bill, but Baby Billy.

I earned the right to become Billy when, at five, I literally jumped off the ground and punched an uncle's nose bloody for calling me Baby Billy. But even after that, I couldn't shed what to my family was some kind of essential weakness. As I pro-gressed through my life, my shortcomings grew right along with me: My tolerance for dope and alcohol was pathetic com-pared to the addicts; I got nervous around the law; was prone to fumble stolen goods when shoplifting; I wouldn't—or, worse, couldn't—shut my girlfriends' mouths; and although I would fight just about anyone, I was absolutely flat-out unable to knock deserving motherfuckers on their asses with a single punch—like, say, my aunt Suzy could.

Outside of my family, I was considered a ruffian. I drove across a neighborhood's worth of front lawns at 50 mph, shot a gun at one of my friends just to prove to him that I would, performed drunken gymnastics on a hotel ledge fifteen stories up. But so profound and incomprehensible was my inherent lacking that at family gatherings I was regarded not with scorn, but with a pity so powerful it approached a kind of awe. Just what in the hell might be wrong with me?

My passion for bicycles was just one more sign of my screwball shortcoming. "Fifty bucks for shoes you can't wear anywhere but on a bicycle!" snorted my uncle Gary, a former member of the Pagans motorcycle gang.

My best friend and I began riding in our senior year of high school. After his parents took his driver's license away as punishment for getting drunk, he bought a racing bike, the lightest, fastest, most exotic two-wheeler I'd ever seen. I've never been able to explain why bicycles captivated me. They are marvels of both the mechanical and the metaphysical. This simple machine, essentially unchanged since its invention more than a hundred years ago, is the most efficient vehicle ever made, converting about 98 percent of the energy put into it into motion. The bicycle is the iconic childhood Christmas present and the star of one of the most powerful rites of passage when, as children, we learn to propel ourselves beyond our parents' reach. Einstein is said to have thought of the theory of relativity while riding. Albert Hofmann, the chemist who accidentally invented the mind-altering drug LSD, rode a bike during the world's first acid trip. A study in the late nineties found that the rhythm of pedaling a bike induces the same physiological changes the body undergoes during intense prayer or meditation.

But for me, the answer—or as close as I ever get to one—is at once simpler and more expansive: The bicycle spoke to my soul. It reached inside me and touched something essential to my spirit the way old stamps, or African violets, or egg tempera infuse other people. Those who pretend to be able to parse the secrets of our primal loves always sound foolish to me. We love what we love, and I love cycling with the same kind of mysterious, infinite delight with which I love Beth and Natalie and nothing else in this world. That is why I ride, because I was a cyclist before I ever saw a bike, the same way I was Beth's husband and Natalie's father before either of them existed for me. That the bicycle as sport was simultaneously alien, effeminate, and intimidating to my childhood family only made my obsession sweeter. I took $500 of the money I'd saved working as a laborer for a bricklayer and bought a used Schwinn Paramount—at the time one of the finest racing bicycles in the world, with wispy wheels, a tiny seat, a lugged-steel frame, and a candy-apple red paint job.

The Paramount helped me find new friends, who were going to college, and once I followed them it helped me graduate: I stayed more sober than I'd thought I would, so I could make most of the big weekend rides, and I tried not to smoke much dope so I'd have the lungs to ride strong. Sometimes, when I knew I'd need the energy for the next day's ride, I even ate right. And in my last quarter of school, I sold that bike to help pay my tuition.

Without exactly knowing what I was doing, I'd more or less

ridden away enough destructive energy to let myself graduate, avoid jail, and meet and romance a farm girl from southern Indiana.

Beth had great legs and a flat, hard stomach and a small, up-curved nose that would have let her be cast as either the princess or the pauper—an endearing flaw if she'd been rich, a hint of better destiny if she'd been penniless, but she was neither, which made the construction of her face all the more enigmatic and alluring. She had a shy tongue, and it seemed to me that she knew nothing of the place from which I'd come. In the flexing and springing of our mutual pursuit, she distanced herself with each flash of my ancestral madness, but became closer and warmer with every quiet act of affection. To her, romance was not a rash leap from the roof of a house, but a rose hidden in the lunch I brought her at work. She'd rather hold my hand than let me go so I could paint her name across the brick wall of the library.

We drank a bottle of wine in a rowboat while arguing about god, then laughed together when, trying to pee into the empty bottle, Beth polluted the shallow bilge of water already washing around our feet. We ordered naked at a barbecue drive-through. We made love in empty classrooms and ravaged each other in stairwells. We went to a pet store pretending to be serious buyers just so we could give a few minutes of play to the deprived animals, and ended up buying a kitten. We fell in love, lived together, got married, and I kept my life intact by riding my bike. I became a successful journalist (eventually the top editor at the world's largest cycling magazine), with a new house on four and a half acres of Pennsylvania woods.

After that crushing miscarriage, our daughter, the innocent and silly and smart and lovely Natalie, was born.

In those years before Natalie, even though I worked at a magazine devoted to bicycles, I was still working—which meant I rode less than I had in high school or college. The old, familiar urges for insanity began seeping into ordinary days. Without context, the transgressions I made could have seemed minor, dismissed as immaturity or a bad temper. There were flirtations that took just a half-step too far before retreating. Once I stole a soda from a convenience store, risking my reputation and dignity for the buck thirty-nine I had in my pocket. I called a nice man who ran the local furniture store a motherfucker—actually, I shouted it a quarter of an inch from his face—because he kept forgetting to order the part that would join our sectional sofa. (On the plus side, our couch was fixed the next day.) But because I had no way to reliably diagnose the severity of my misdeeds, each mistake felt like a bend in the bar of a cage holding an awful beast.

I could no longer ride enough to protect my wife, and my life, so I started relying on the sheer doggedness I must have learned or inherited from my mother. As a shrink once said to me, "You don't instinctively and naturally know right from wrong. You have to stop and think about it—you're morally groundless, and the fact that you've gone this long without destroying yourself is a testament to your willpower. You've willed yourself to do the right things."

Sometimes I'd have to stop myself four or five times a day from doing something amoral; sometimes I'd go a week without incident, but always I lived in a state of readiness against the impulses that threatened to obliterate my life.

In 1998, when Natalie was born, what had been anticipation became terror. I obsessively, fearfully monitored my smallest actions and thoughts for any wisp of wrongdoing. When I was tired and irritated at 3 A.M., carrying Natalie on my shoulder and singing nonsense to her, I had no way of knowing if I was just tired and irritated like a normal father or if that was the emotion that would lead us down into hell. Hitting her, harming her, torturing her seemed unimaginable to me, but the things that had happened to me as a child had been unimaginable. I loved Natalie with a fresh, complete, and boundless wonder that expanded and deepened daily, hourly, by the minute—I loved her like a father. I was afraid of loving her like my father.

I fought the thing inside me and rode when I could, as much as I could, as much as a responsible husband with a new daughter and what felt like an important job could manage. And when I couldn't ride, I was terrified. I could feel something stirring inside my chest, awakening from the sleep that cycling fatigued it into. It stretched and reached out and tickled the inside of my skin, not as if it wanted to rip its way out, but teasing me with a nearly erotic touch, a caress that promised the sweetness of release.

six

W ITH THIRTEEN LAPS LEFT IN THE FIFTH C RIT, J ACK
Simes insinuated himself into a space I hadn't known existed.
His front wheel appeared between the blurring parallel circles
made by my feet and the rider to my right. An inch either way,
and our pedals would have shredded the spokes from Simes's
wheel. The left drop of his handlebar slid forward across my
hip. His shoulder did not so much bump mine as appear off of
it like a shadow, then there was a quick movement and my
shoulder had become the shadow as his became the dominant,
real, material thing.

Despite his elegance, there in the middle of the ninety-two-
racer pack—the biggest of the season—I almost didn't recognize Simes. I thought he must have been someone who looked
like himself, because the real Jack Simes III was ordained to sit
up front. His father, Jack Simes II, was the 1936 national road
champion. Jack III had gone to three Olympics and eight

world championships (where he'd once finished second), had won nine national championships, and set three different American cycling records. He was a short, wiry man with white hair and a craggy face, and thin white calves streaked with black, red, and purple veins. Off the bike, you'd call him irascible. In the saddle of his ancient, white steel Colnago, he was poetry; he rode with a lyricism just about anyone could appreciate but that regular people couldn't really follow.

I caught his wheel, popping a hard and crude elbow to drive off my twin, the other rider who'd been displaced so artfully, and just as the hole that Simes had opened in front of us began slamming shut, I fit myself through. With his slight, yet unopposable grace, a style that created rather than exploited breaches, Simes started transferring us through the pack faster than I had imagined was possible. He never had to pause to look for an opening or plan a route. He just birthed and passed through gap after gap after gap. And each time he vanished into the wall of riders in front of us, I clenched my teeth and sprinted after him. Twice there was the slithery zinging sound of wheels touching wheels. Once I smelled burnt rubber.

Simes sat up. We were at the front, in a group of about twelve. There was Torch—Bruce Donaghy—a six-time national champ who'd been a member of the Boycott Olympics team in 1980. There was Bobby Lea, the kid, the new national champion of the kilometer, a timed solo race called the "killometer" because it's generally agreed to be the most physically excruciating single minute in cycling. There was fifteen-year-old Jackie Simes IV, the youngest of the dynasty. There was Sarah Uhl, a twenty-year-old national champ. The Animal. A local pro called Speedy—one of those people about whom others, when asked if they liked him, would say, "I respect him." There was Art the Dart McHugh, a goofy, lovable Jekyll with a Hyde sprint. There was Gibby the Bear Hatton, who'd coached Marty Nothstein to a gold medal in the match sprint at the 2000 Olympics and who, legend held, before retiring had made a fortune as the dirtiest, meanest superstar villain ever in keirin—a Japanese form of velodrome racing in which spectators gamble on cyclists as if they are horses.

As a group, they already had more than a hundred points between them on the season.

Gibby moved alongside me, crowding me with his thigh, his forearm, elbow, shoulder, and even with his breath. He pushed me sideways off Simes. It was a forceful, cruel, crushing, and unstoppable move—but steady and fair. I dangled half in Simes's draft and half out in the wind. The left side of my face could feel the heat emanating from Gibby's grizzly bulk. The right side was chilled by the spring wind.

I swallowed and kicked up my cadence and got ready to lay myself into the Bear—to push him sideways so I could take back Simes's wheel. Gibby moved me over again. Some invisible, undetectable flick I'd never felt had put me fully out in the wind. My eyes stung. I put a furious effort into my cadence and hit 130 rpm, more than two pedal strokes a second. Beside me, tucked into the pack, Gibby was coasting. I popped against his shoulder and bounced back off.

There was no way through him. I sat up to begin drifting back to the soft middle of the pack, where I could burrow in to hide from the wind.

The bell rumbled into us.

We'd crossed the line to start a points lap. As if I were

following Simes to a destination I couldn't see, I stood and stomped a pedal, blindly shooting forward. The bell was still banging as the twelve of us skittered into the first corner. I stayed up on my pedals, and when I flicked my eyes to the left there was no one beside me. I was alone, off the front.

All alone. I sat, but kept my feet going. I blew all the air out of my lungs. I looked back. You were not supposed to. You were supposed to ride off as if you didn't need to look back. The pack was 15 feet behind me. I accelerated all the way to the twisty approach to the hill then pounced again out of the saddle, smashing my legs onto the pedals. The crest of the hill shook from side to side, as if an earthquake had struck. Something scalding and sulphurous filled my throat. I sat down trembling and snuck a peek back. Bobby Lea was on my wheel.

I yawed over to the left and he came past me and I looked down and to the right and saw Sarah Uhl behind him. As she rode up beside me, I could see her looking over, studying me, trying to figure out who I was, this heaving, hurting guy out in front of the pack. She tipped her head up once at me, half a nod. I gave her a half-nod back, and she flicked out a smile that fell somewhere between an acknowledgment and a welcome.

I slid back and fell in behind her. Bobby pulled to the top of the hill, then heeled left and began drifting back and Sarah took the lead. As Bobby went by, he looked over at me and I looked over at him, thinking it might be unnerving to bluff my face into the same look Sarah had had on hers: So who are you?

Bobby Lea grinned. It was a genuine, young, toothy bright smile full of energy and careless elation. The kid was having a blast.

Our speed washed us forward. We surfed atop a towering,

deafening wave of momentum of our own making. Within a few pedal strokes, the pavement began rushing under our wheels as if we were hovering motionless over a mad river. Then, weightless entirely, we felt ourselves loosed from the puny forces of gravity and propulsion. Down the hill and through the curves with one national champion ahead of me and another behind, we were free, light, pure light. We were faster than light, and as boundless. Then Sarah flapped her right elbow, letting me know she was done, and she pulled over to the left and the wind smashed into my face.

I didn't cry when he broke my nose with a hammer. I was behind him, leaning against his shoulder as he squatted over whatever it was we were working on out there in the garage, the thing that had become that day's pivotal match against the world that wanted to beat us into submission. A bolt that had rusted stuck, a store that demanded too much for a pair of pants, the boss who required sobriety, the bigger and older fourth-grader who scared me—they were all the same battle for my father.

"Fuck it," he said and, without rising from his squat, he turned at the waist and brought the hammer around and, almost casually, popped me between the eyes.

There was a strobe flash of light. A single sharp snap. An immediate, internal sense of something coming apart. Narrow, wet, scalding lines drilled down both sides of my nose.

My father stood. He looked down, chewed one side of his mouth, and studied me. The weight of the hammer in his hand swung his arm in tight little pendulums. I could taste the metal tang of the tool at the back of my throat.

The hot flow widened, spread sticky and shallow and cooler

across my cheeks. I reached up, dipped my index finger against my face then tilted it backward, filling half my field of vision with red. I moved my hand up to the bridge of my nose to press myself back together. The top of my nose, where it was supposed to attach to my forehead, moved up, down, in.

I did not cry. I waited to see if my father might somehow turn this into a joke. He could make a lot of things funny.

At the end of one of the hammer's backward arcs, he released it and it clattered onto something metal behind him then clunked blunt onto the concrete floor.

"We have to clean this up," he said.

In the bathroom, he set me up on the sink. Blood began wicking down my T-shirt and flowing faster and squiggly along the skin of my chest into the waistband of my jeans. I brought my legs together so my thighs would catch the blood that dripped off my nose and chin whenever I leaned forward.

My father took a stack of towels from the closet and piled them on the counter. When my mother did laundry, she'd fold each washcloth into the center of a matching towel. My father opened a towel, pulled out a washcloth, and unfurled it and held it up. It was straggly on the edges and thin enough to see light through in the middle. He refolded it, laid it back in the towel, and closed the towel on itself again and set it aside. He opened another towel, rejected the washcloth and packed it shut, and set it aside and opened another.

Another. Another, each examination meticulous and patient, the towels in two neat towers, and finally he found a washcloth he wanted, a soft, thick, blue one, as if that was our family's broken-nose washcloth, the one we retrieved every time someone's nose got smashed with a hammer.

My father ran the faucet hot, soaked the cloth in the steaming water, and wrung it out and laid it against my nose, soft and warm and tender, and it was then that I cried, a single throat-bruising sob that pushed out of me like vomit and opened the way for a long, trilling wail that pulsed out of me like blood, on and on and on. I cried because it hurt, and because I was loved, and because there was no way anymore to separate the two.

I gasped for breath under the crush of the wind, then got tossed backward. Sarah Uhl and Bobby Lea rode away, kids playing, down the hill and into the woods, their whole lives ahead of them, this lap nothing but one more romp temporarily enlivened by a puzzling, intense man who'd suddenly blown up less than half a mile away from getting points, and who would be forgotten by next week if not tonight. The good guys whistled past me, and then the rest of the field, and I tucked into them, determined not to abandon in the woods again. But I couldn't even keep up back there, amid the softest, weakest part of the pack, where no one had any chance at all of going fast while they were smiling.

seven

"IT'S EARLY," SAID BETH. "FIVE RACES IS NOT A SEA-
son." She picked up the bottle of wine that sat in the middle of
the small round table of our favorite Italian restaurant, and
splashed my glass half full of liquid that was the color and
opacity of the red cellophane in 3-D goggles.

An amusing sensory association was as sophisticated as my
wine palate got. Beth knew the name, the winery, the vintage,
and the major critics' ratings of every bottle we drank. Since
she had become a budding wine connoisseur in the past year,
one of the reasons we tried to make a date for dinner at Louie's
at least once a month was that it was BYOB, and Beth pre-
ferred to drink from her own collection. Early on in her new
hobby, she'd gone for expensive bottles, but had quickly gotten bored with that. "Of course I can get us a great wine for
eighty bucks," she'd said. She'd decided to concentrate on
pursuing wines that got top ratings from critics but cost less

than $25. The knowledge that a wine was rated a 90 and had cost $19, and the rigors of the chase that had led her to the bottle, seemed to be as influential to her pleasure as the actual taste of the wine. She cataloged her outstanding catches, and on the labels of the bottles stored in our tiny wine refrigerator, she noted information such as the rating—a habit my friend Steak made fun of whenever we had him and his wife over for dinner. I knew that marking up labels betrayed our lack of sophistication. But it sure made picking a wine easy.

So I had to give some weight to the math my wife was presenting me with during our date the night after the Crit: Five races plus zero points equals zero significance. Looking across the table at Beth's face, the surety there, I suddenly did feel as if my five failed attempts at racing had been nothing but a warm-up. My chances to score stretched out away from this night, farther than I could see, a summer-long string of so many opportunities that I was foolish to fret about something so inconsequential as the fact that I couldn't even hang onto the pack. Depending on the weather, I had as many as twenty more races—600 laps. And, of those, 200 that counted—200 sprint laps, 200 chances to score. Out of that bounty, I needed to cross the finish line in fourth place a mere ten times. Or cross third twice, and fourth six times. Or somehow pull off a second, or . . .

"Stop," said Beth. "Cease all thinking about ten points." She reached across the table and forked some of the chunks of gorgonzola cheese off my salad. After she popped them into her mouth and swallowed, she said, "I can't believe there was a time when I didn't like salad."

"The hazards of a meat-and-potatoes childhood," I said. "I

can't believe you used to think I was some kind of chef because I poured Chunky Soup on top of rice—"

"And called it Chinese food." Beth wrinkled her nose at the culinary deception I'd perpetrated when we first started hanging out with each other at Ball State. Her mouth had a wonderful way of looking unkempt, as if she'd just gotten up from bed, at any time of day. "I still can't believe you forced yourself to like tomatoes."

I said, "Willpower." In my early thirties, I'd decided that if I ate tomatoes eight straight times I'd end up being able to at least tolerate them. "What I can't believe is that after a lifetime of being disgusted by strawberries, I loved them the first time you put one in my mouth." That had been on our fifth wedding anniversary.

"Oh, that was delight," Beth said. "It's so much more powerful than will."

A waitress appeared and spirited away our salad bowls. Another one conjured steaming mounds of linguine in front of each of us, milled fresh parmesan into our heaping bowls, and vanished. The small room around us murmured with date-night talk. An air conditioner or a dehumidifier kicked on. Silverware clinked.

In one of those episodes that I now recognized as a necessary step in courtship, but which at the time felt like a terminal diagnosis, Beth had decided that even though she loved me, when she graduated from college she wanted to try out life without me around. She had moved to Olympia, Washington. I'd stayed in Indiana to finish my last few classes—I hadn't been as diligent as her about carrying a full load every quarter—and to make the most of my broken heart. She'd called one day and asked me to pick up a box she'd left behind at her great-grandfather's house, down in the southern Indiana farmland. The rambling, three-story brick house was falling apart, but had once been a mansion—by Indiana hick standards, at least. Inside, it was dominated by the kind of broad, sweeping staircase you saw in movies, and there was fancy gingerbread-work all over the outside, a cavernous fireplace, and even a few hidden rooms and tunnels up on the top floor. Her great-grandfather lived there with her father and a pack of bitter dogs, a few miles from the farm her family had owned when she was a kid. There was a cornfield out back that stretched to the horizon, but it no longer belonged with the house; her great-grandfather kept a garden out back of the collapsing barn.

When I crunched onto the gravel driveway, the dogs ran out to see if they could bring down the car. You could hear their teeth clinking off the fenders. One leaped up and smashed his mouth in sideways profile against the window. I sat and waited.

After a minute or so, the porch door opened and Papaw stuck his head out. He saw it was me, and walked out onto the faded green slats of the porch. "What are you doing sitting out there?" he shouted. He was taller than me, and thinner, had pure white hair and moved like someone pretending to be an old person, as if he was hoping to let you in on the joke. I opened the car door and stepped out, and the dogs ran over and licked my hands. One of them jumped up and licked my cheek. I never knew if they accepted my presence once Papaw gave his assent, or if they simply enjoyed embarrassing me.

Papaw stood on the porch and watched me walk toward him with dogs swirling around me, his expression that of a parent watching one of those school plays where the set falls down around the hopelessly earnest kid. I went up the steps, put a hand on the rail, and said, "Beth asked me to pick up a box and send it out to her."

"Hell," he said, "I don't know what all boxes are here. Help me shell these beans." He gestured to a five-gallon bucket filled with little snips of green. He scootched a rocking chair next to the bucket, then walked over and got a stool and set it on the other side of the beans and sat down on it. He reached in and picked up a bean and shelled it. He threw part of it in another bucket then pitched another part, which looked like the shredded paper of an unwrapped present, into a paper grocery sack that had been rolled into a cuff at the top. He reached in and got another bean and looked up at me.

I sat down in the rocking chair and picked up a bean. I didn't know what to do with it. I held it and watched his hands, but I couldn't track their movements. There were three crisp snaps. Two pieces of green bean arced into the keeper bucket. The bean felt fuzzy in my hands, full of life. There was something shockingly sensual about the seam that ran its length. I'd never held a fresh green bean, just pulled from the garden.

Papaw was looking at me. His fingers deliberately snapped off each end of the long bean, then pulled a string up from each side and snapped the bean in half. He flipped his beans into the bucket, discarded the waste, and pulled out another.

I snapped off the ends, then fumbled with the strings. They broke before I could pull them all the way off. I kept at it. I heard Papaw's beans bounce off the side of the bucket, and then another pair. Snaps came from his direction. Crickets chirped and out in the yard, the dogs savaged each other with happy snarls. It was the kind of warm evening that carried little pockets of cool into us.

I looked at Papaw and said, "I don't know what the hell I'm doing."

He nodded and smiled. "Shit, son, I know that." More beans plonked off the bucket. Cracks and snaps. Papaw said, "You going after her?"

I snapped my bean in half, and threw in my first two contributions. "I don't think she wants to be chased right now."

"I think you know what you're doing there," Papaw said.

I picked up another bean and was startled all over again by its fuzziness. "Sometimes," I said, "I think it's possible to chase a woman by running away from her."

"Maybe sometimes," Papaw said. He pinched his nostrils between his thumb and forefinger, then swiped his hand across the pant leg of his denim overalls. "But not this girl." He pulled a bean out of the bucket and turned around, and used the vegetable to gesture out to the garden by the barn. "You see that rabbit there?"

I looked into the stripped stalks and fallen leaves of the garden and shook my head no. Papaw waggled the bean and I looked closer and saw a furry patch of light brown against some browned stalks. I wondered how he'd seen the rabbit with his back turned. He said, "You or me neither could chase that rabbit down, nor get it to chase us." He flicked his wrist and the bean he'd been holding flew out across the yard, whirling like a boomerang, and fell at the edge of the garden. The rabbit startled and froze.

We watched it for a little bit. It never moved.

"It's not going for the bean," I said, thinking, "Some parable."

Papaw shook his head, and picked out a new bean and shelled it, then threw the waste away and tossed the two good pieces into the bag. "Shell these beans," he said. "When we're done, you walk out there and see if that one ain't been taken."

The bean had been gone when I'd left, without the box I was supposed to pick up. When I'd gotten home that night, I'd written Beth a letter that was, for the first time, neither a diatribe nor a manifesto. I'd written her a letter every day after that. They'd been simple, funny letters about shelling beans, about life in Indiana.

"I can't believe you came back to me," I said.

Beth was twirling her fork into her linguine and she stopped. She said, "I had to." That might have been true of her return to the Midwest, but when she looked down, into her bowl, and didn't look back up even when I knew she had to feel me staring across the table at her, I knew she was thinking of another time.

"I meant back to Indiana," I said. "When we were in college. I was thinking of delight. The thing that brought you back then. You know—delight is much more powerful than will."

"Oh."

I stared into my wineglass and waited for the liquid to look like something to me. In curved reflection I saw Beth bring her fork toward her mouth. From the concave inside of the wineglass, Beth paused, waggled her fork at me, and, attempting to salvage date night, said, "It's really delicious tonight. Besides, you have to eat if you want to score ten points."

But on that, her math was all wrong.

* * *

As much as I believed that scoring ten points was about heart, I could not ignore the fact that it was also about math. For years, with the advent of lab testing and genetic detectiveship, success in cycling had been quantifiable in figures and formulas. These equations weren't known and celebrated by the general public—and probably shouldn't be. Fans wanted to be awed by Lance Armstrong's intangible heart, not by the stroke volume of the beating muscle itself. Yet, as I searched for every edge my body would give me, I found myself uncharacteristically turning into a numbers geek. There was an enticing simplicity to working out the bewildering and uncharted boundaries of my quest as if they could be solved with a calculator.

The bodies of the best cyclists in the world, such as Armstrong, produce an amount of power equal to just about 2.5 watts per pound of their total weight. Average pros and world-class amateurs, like those found at the Thursday Crit, generate around 1.8 to 2 watts per pound. Thanks to a special computer I'd briefly ridden with—one that measures not just speed but how much force you put into your pedal stroke—I knew that I was puttering along at about 240 total watts, or just about 1.6 per pound. I also knew, thanks to some tests I'd done with physiologists at the start of the season, that I was never going to be able to consistently produce much more wattage. The tests had measured my current strength, resting heart rate, maximum heart rate, and VO2 max (how much oxygen I could take in and process), and predicted ceilings for each number. The verdict: Genetically I was phenomenally, spectacularly ordinary.

It was the VO2 max in particular that doomed me. That number's high point is determined by our DNA. How close we get to it is up to us. For instance, at the peak of his training,

Armstrong's VO2 max had been measured at 81.2, according to physiologists who'd studied him—nearly all of his potential. My VO2 max was 61—and that was about all I had, too, which put me in the genetically average person's range of 56–62. (For further confirmation of my physical mediocrity, if needed, I could contemplate the fact that if Armstrong stopped riding, and sat on a couch watching cartoons and eating donuts, his predicted genetic low would be somewhere between 61 and 63, or the highest I could ever reach no matter how diligently I trained.)

Although my engine couldn't get much bigger, my chassis could get smaller; I couldn't boost watts much, but I could increase my watt-per-pound ratio by losing weight.

At five foot nine and 150, I was by no means fat. I was, in fact, already somewhere beyond lean. My 150 pounds were not balanced out across my body in a typical way. As my legs had become layered with muscle, and thus heavier, I'd shrunk up top. I was hollow-cheeked and twig-armed, and friends who hadn't seen me in a while would ask if I'd been sick—which was a good sign, because fast cyclists look ill.

But none of that was enough. For what I wanted to accomplish, in the realm I was trying to ride in, I was fat. If I ever wanted a chance at scoring points, I had to get down into the low 140s—while also harvesting whatever slight increase in power my body would yield. I figured I had a shot at 1.65 or 1.7 watts per pound—still not world class, but good enough to tuck in behind world class, and maybe good enough to hope to get lucky in the last 50 feet before a sprint line.

So I'd begun starving myself. Except for race day, when I would loose my appetite upon our kitchen's pasta-heavy cupboards and the town's Italian restaurants, I survived on stingy amounts of protein and simple carbohydrates. When I arose for my 5 A.M. base rides, I would drink a double espresso (taking on faith a study I'd read that claimed caffeine increased the body's ability to burn fat while exercising mildly), then get on my bike. I'd ride one hour without eating, have one banana during the second hour, then come home and have a banana and a piece of toast, or a serving of cereal tiny enough to fit in my palm. I'd ride again at noon on my lunch break, then afterward refuel with a dollop of peanut butter, some egg whites, and a fist-sized bowl of pasta.

I was embarrassed when I ordered my lunch in the office cafeteria beside the other people who'd also ridden that day but were eating what they could and should—heaping plates of pasta, ham sandwiches, tortilla chips, and brownies. For nearly a month, my head had been vibrating with a buzzing hum all the time I was awake. I learned that a hungry person's mouth does literally water at the sight of a full plate. My boss began calling me "amazingly lifelike." By the first of May, my senses had begun to scramble and overlap. One day, some papers on my desk smelled like ripe apples. A few days later, I picked up a pen and dropped it because it felt as if I'd grabbed a wet spaghetti noodle.

Another day at work, Steak and I were jabbering in my office when his intern walked by the door on the way to the copier. She was in her twenties, with a fresh, chubby curviness like a piece of fruit about to burst. Her stomach protruded between her belly-shirt and jeans as if it had split them at a seam.

"Oh man," I said.

"Come on," said Steak.

"I want to eat her."

"Dude!" He looked out the door and back at me. "What the fuck?"

"No—wait, hang on," I sputtered. "Not like that. I mean, I want to really eat her. I flashed on this image of myself carving out a piece of her thigh."

"Oh my god," said Steak.

My mouth was watering, going dry, watering. "I want to take her to a motel and sit her on a Magic Fingers bed and watch her eat chocolate syrup from a bowl with her fingers," I said, as if that were less disturbing than proposing cunnilingus with the intern. "I want to buy her flowers and give them to her in a heaping bucket of Kentucky Fried Chicken."

"I hope you're getting faster," said Steak.

I was getting faster, but the stress of doing so was beginning to tear both me and my bike apart. My legs ached. I had trouble walking down stairs. I rode with an ongoing barrage of saddle sores—oozy wounds opened up on my butt from hours of chafing. My bike's bolts were loosening, its chain was stretching, the tires were showing threads and cracks. For the past two weeks, my bike had announced its suffering with an ongoing series of squeaks, rattles, groans, ticks, thumps, creaks, moans, and chirps.

I fixed the obvious mechanical problems as they arose, but the arcane art of finding and eliminating mysterious noises was like trying to cure cancer in a Neanderthal cave. Mechanics in bike shops deplore and fear the bike that comes in because "it's making a funny noise."

For professional advice, I relied on Taylor, who worked at South Mountain Cycles, a bike and espresso shop in the central triangle of our small town. Taylor and the owner, Mark, drew short, stiff cups of espresso out of a machine manufactured by Faema, the company that had sponsored the team of the great Eddy Merckx in the early seventies. Taylor was wild-haired and supernaturally lean, and festooned his face with goatees, handlebar moustaches, ironic mutton-chops, and other expressions of his mood. He was somewhere between eighteen and forty, had probably looked that age his whole life and would continue on ageless, appearing ever in his prime until some magic day late in his life when he'd instantly transform into one of those ancient, crumpled mechanics who sit at the workstands in bike shops like gurus on mountaintops. He was funny and manic one day, then serene the next, but no matter what his current bearing was, he could engage anyone from the three-year-old who was scared of the new bike she was getting, to the world champion who needed a wheel built, to the rich weight-weenie who wanted a 15-pound bike that would never travel faster than 15 mph. He was, at least outwardly, enthusiastically living a life focused on a calling that, like a teacher or social worker or nursing-home caregiver, was important but doomed by market forces to a wage most Americans would find untenable, if not unlivable. In terms of bike repair, his breadth of knowledge was as wide as a family doctor's, his depth as total as a brain surgeon's. He was a wrench—the purest expression of the bike mechanic.

My dream of ten points was in his greasy hands.

"It stopped ticking," I said to Taylor, wheeling my LOOK down three steps from street-level into the South Mountain Cycles shop. "Now it's tocking." It was eight in the morning. After date night, I'd gotten up at 5:30 to ride.

"Doppio?" he asked, walking to the Faema, and I nodded. The beans ground, and he began drawing down a double espresso roughly the consistency of motor oil. "It's probably the seat again. But it could be the pedals. Or the crankarms. Or the bottom bracket or the chainring bolts or loose cogs or the front or rear wheel."

"Yeah," I said. "That's what I thought."

"Or something else." He handed me a tiny glass cup. Noises, we both knew, notoriously travel throughout bikes. A click from the front wheel can manifest itself in the saddle. A creaky saddle can sound and even feel as if the crankset is loose. The most superstitious cyclists believe that noises can travel between bikes as well—ride too long near a creaking bike and the sound waves infect yours.

"What do you think I should try?"

Taylor kneeled beside my bike, stretched one hand up to the saddle, and fluttered the fingers of his other hand along the smooth carbon tubes. "You're not gonna wanna hear this," he said, then frowned. "But if I were you, I'd take the whole thing apart and do a fresh build."

That night, I began to completely disassemble my bike, planning to remove every piece of metal from the frame, even the headset, a pair of bearing cups that are press-fit into the bike and must be removed and installed with special, unwieldy tools that look like medieval torture instruments.

Natalie sat out in the bike room watching me and changing CDs as I scrubbed parts with citrus degreaser and an old toothbrush. My home shop was a separate, third garage the original owner had built. When we'd moved in four years earlier, I'd screwed bike hooks to the walls and wheel hooks to the ceiling, nailed plywood to two walls and pounded nails halfway into the sheets to hold my tools. There's a sink, an electric floorboard heater, an exhaust fan, a cheap boombox and my ten-year-old, shop-quality repair stand. The cluttered, dirty room fascinated Natalie.

She watched me unbolt the saddle from the seatpost I'd removed from the bike earlier. I separated the seat clamp into three pieces and, standing over the sink, began to clean them.

"Daddy," said Natalie. "So what is wrong with your seat?" She was standing beside my bike, which was mounted in the stand. The chain was on the small ring in front, so the teeth of the big, outer ring were exposed, and she was touching each one in turn with her right index finger, hard enough to leave an indentation that lasted for two or three seconds after she took her finger off. She watched the depressions in her skin fill themselves.

"Careful, Boo," I said.

She stopped pressing her finger against the chainring teeth.

I said, "It's not a seat. It's a saddle."

Natalie began to run her finger over the surface of the chain. I knew how it felt—slick from the lube, yet not wet, and the roller pins between each link would spin under her finger and tickle her. She said, "Daddy. You cannot ride a horse with that saddle."

"Nope."

I set the clamp pieces down on a rag I'd spread out on the workbench, sprayed a clean rag with degreaser, then walked a couple of steps over to the bike and stuffed the cloth inside the tube where the seatpost goes. I twirled the rag around and pulled it out. Natalie had moved out of my way, toward the front of the bike, and before I could say anything she latched her finger over one of the spokes of the front wheel, then yanked her hand down. The thirty-two distinct spokes instantly transformed into a flickering platter of silver, and as Nat pulled her hand away, several of the spokes thunked her knuckle.

"Dammit, Nat!" I barked.

She was flapping her hand as if she'd touched a hot stove.

"Are you hurt?" I asked, reaching for her hand. As the words had started to come out of my mouth, I could tell that my voice would sound more angry than concerned, but I'd been unable to change the tone.

She shook her head and half-turned, putting one of her tiny shoulders between me and the hand she was still flopping. She said, "No."

I took two deep breaths. I said, "You could break your finger that way."

"I didn't." She was ready for bed, in a blue gown on which all sorts of cats romped about. A hem of white, frilly fringe swept the floor of the bike shop as she bobbed her knees in time with the shaking of her hand. I knew that she thought I might send her to bed for being careless, and that was outweighing the sting of her knuckles.

"You're okay?" I said. She nodded, and I said, "Don't touch anything without asking. I want you to be able to mess around with the bike when we're out here and figure out how it works and everything but you have to ask—or you'll get hurt. Bad." I stared at her for punctuation.

"I know."

"A bike can be pretty dangerous."

"Daddy." A big sigh. "I know." She was an expert at reading the intensity and flow of my parenting patterns, and now just wanted to end this obviously uneventful sequence. For a moment I was tempted to send her to bed just to knock her knowledge of me off balance for future advantage.

Instead I said, "Okay," though I wasn't sure what I was agreeing to. I began stuffing the rag back down into the hollow tube of the bike frame.

Natalie asked, "Is that what's wrong with your bike?"

"It could be," I said. "This is called the seat tube. The noise also might be coming from the seatpost." I pulled the rag out; it was no dirtier than when it had gone in. The seat tube wasn't the problem.

"No, Daddy. This is a joke. I meant is what's wrong with your saddle that you can't ride a horse with it?"

"You're funny, Boo," I said. I walked back over to the bench and picked up the clamp pieces and began inspecting them for corrosion or embedded grit.

"For real life. How come it's not called a saddle-post?"

"How come," I said, "my daughter can be so smart but stick her fingers into a spinning wheel?"

"Can I turn the pedals?"

"Yeah," I said. I thought I saw a speck of something on one of the serrated surfaces of the clamp. I brought it closer to my eyes and studied it. "Just keep your other hand away from the chainrings while they're spinning." I reached for a tiny awl I kept on my workbench for the sole purpose of picking out grit from tight spaces. I said, "They can cut a finger off." I heard the pedals turn and the chain meshing with the teeth of the chainrings up front and the cogs in back, that sibilant metal whisper I loved.

I poked at the black speck and realized it was not grit, just a splotch of grease that had long ago been absorbed into the metal and thus could not vibrate between metal pieces or keep them apart so they could rattle and create the noise I'd been hearing. I said, "Shit," and I glanced over at Nat.

She was cranking around the pedals with her right hand. As directed, her left hand was nowhere near the chainrings. It was suspended over the top run of chain. She was letting her index finger tap down on the chain so it would briefly skim along the surface of her skin and tickle her. As she did this, the chain was carrying her finger forward—toward the spinning teeth of the chainrings. I'd been cleaning a bike once, gotten careless, and let my finger get pulled into the junction of the teeth and the chain, and by the time my digit had worked its way around the circle the metal had cut all the way through my fingernail and halfway through my flesh.

"Natalie!"

She looked at me, but kept spinning the pedals, kept letting her finger get pulled toward the teeth. I lunged at her and batted her left arm away from the bike, catching her hard in the crook of her elbow with the seat clamp pieces in my hand. She stumbled backward and banged into the cabinet where I kept spare tires, and I said, "Goddammit. What'd I tell you? What'd I tell you?"

Then I was holding her, my arms on either side of her shoulders, and I was shaking her, then squeezing her, being careful somehow to not get my greasy hands on her favorite nightgown. "I'm sorry, I'm sorry, I'm sorry, I'm sorry," I said as she cried.

eight

THE NEXT MORNING, ON A SUNNY SPRING SUNDAY WITH a summer temperature in the high sixties, Natalie and I rolled around the parking lot of the Crit course trying to decide who else's dream we could make come true. I was pedaling a beater five-speed I usually only used to putter around town, pulling Natalie behind me on her tow-bike—one of those contraptions that instead of a front wheel had a clamp that hooked onto my seatpost to link us.

"Daddy. Her," said Natalie. I looked over my left shoulder. Nat had her left hand off the handlebar and was pointing at an overweight woman in her forties who was smoking a cigarette and standing beside a bike that looked even older. The woman saw Natalie pointing and me staring. I took my left hand off the bar and waved. Unbalanced, our coupled bikes dipped right. I returned my hand to the bar, shot a look forward to make sure our line was clear, and looked back at Natalie again.

"Don't point, Boo," I said.

Natalie waved. "But we can wave."

We swept right, around the parking lot's grassy median, and the woman slid out of our view. I started pedaling again and within two or three strokes could feel that Natalie wasn't pedaling. "Spin," I said. "We need to warm up."

Natalie said something the wind knocked away from my ears. I turned my head and, over my shoulder, reminded her to speak up. Then, affecting a deliberately hyperpedantic tone I used sometimes when I laid life's heaviest stuff on her, I said, "On bikes, Riffo, the leaders are effortlessly loud and clear, while those in back must clamor just to be noticed, let alone understood."

"What?"

"You have to speak up."

"Okay."

I felt a satisfying little burst of wattage nudge my bike forward, and I knew she was pedaling. My bike was surprisingly sensitive to the input that came from hers, whether it was power or wobbles telegraphed through the frame when she moved around.

I said, "So what did you say?"

"I said okay."

"Before that."

She'd stopped pedaling. She said, "That's when I said what you couldn't hear."

"I know that."

"Okay, Daddy. Good."

I stopped pedaling too, and as we coasted, my freehub clicked us down the length of the parking lot. When we carved a lazy right around the other end of the median, I said, "So Natalie, what did you say?"

"I said okay again."

When I looked back, she was smiling. Her miniature, maroon cycling jersey was being pulled tight backward and off her shoulders by the weight of the two Mike & Ike candy boxes that had come in the goody bags we'd gotten at the registration table earlier that morning. Her black spandex bike shorts sagged loose on her skinny thighs. Her blue helmet, with its monochromatic flower prints, tilted adorably off to one side. One of her cycling gloves was unfastened at the wrist strap.

I said, "Okay, Natalie. What was the first thing you said, since we've been riding this morning, that I couldn't hear?"

"I said what do you think her dream is?"

I'd been unable to convince Natalie that the Dream Come True charity ride functioned solely to raise money that funded the fulfillment of ill people's wishes. She understood that the money we cyclists donated was used for this purpose, but she also believed that the act of cycling itself somehow fueled the enterprise—that, as far as I could comprehend, our ride was the spark that allowed the money to burn in service of the dream. The money simply wouldn't work without the riding. It was vital, therefore, that we select a person whose dream we would ride into being. This was especially important in our specific case because, Natalie believed, we were going to win the ride.

I'd also been unable to convince her that you can't take first place in a charity ride.

"We're going to win," Natalie had announced to the white-haired woman running the registration booth that morning.

The woman had chuckled, looked at me to share the joke, and said, "Well, we're all winners, aren't we?"

"No," said Natalie. "Just the first four across the line. I have new pedals with rubber strips so my shoes don't slip anymore."

We were passing by the cigarette woman again. I said, "I don't think she's one of the dreamers, Nat. I don't think she's sick. Yet."

On our next loop, I braked us to a stop in front of the Pepsi trailer that served as command central. It was 10 A.M. and our 15-mile ride started in a few minutes. Beth and some friends had left at 8:30 to do the long route. Over a portable PA, a woman began giving us advice about the route, about how to follow the markers that had been spray-painted onto the local roads, and how to ride safely in traffic. There were maybe twenty cyclists in our group: some old people, some moms and dads on neglected bikes alongside kids four or five years older than Nat on heavy, department-store BMXers and pink bikes with streamers fluttering from the handlebars.

"Daddy!" She was shouting to be heard over the announcer.

"Yeah?"

"We can beat all these people."

An old man, maybe in his sixties, on a bike with a step-through woman's frame, narrowed his eyes at me, and near him a twenty-something kid, fit but not a cyclist, on a dusty mountain bike, stared over at us. Two of the eight-ish boys said something to each other. It didn't seem as if they could have heard Nat, but I turned and told her, "You have to be careful what you say on a start line."

My daughter appraised all of them with an Animal-cool gaze, then turned to me, pursed her lips, and gave a single nod.

During this little drama, the announcer had been introducing two kids whose dreams had come true in the past thanks to this event, and I missed most of the details. One of them was a girl who'd been serving sodas in the trailer, a freshman in college who waved shyly out at the riders. She was cute, but in some indistinct character of her muscular structure, she was obviously a survivor of some dread disease. The other girl, who had gone to Disney, was younger, maybe ten. She wore her illness in the hollows and edges of her face, with a blank look and a heaviness in her eyes.

The announcer sent us off. Within two pedal strokes, I knew that Natalie's bragging had been overheard and the start-line stare-down hadn't been my imagination. We were no longer the only ones racing the charity ride. The two kids sprinted off the line, leaving the parents fumbling to get both feet on their pedals. The old man shot past us, contorted into an impossible aerodynamic hunch over a handlebar raised higher than his saddle. The young guy on the mountain bike eyeballed me as he passed unnecessarily close.

I wasn't dressed like a cyclist, let alone a racer. Three-quarter-length pants, the kind urban bike messengers wear, hid my spandex bike shorts from view. I was wearing shoes designed for bike touring; their thick soles enabled me to walk without clacking along on the embedded cleats. I'd chosen a jersey that was baggy, without back pockets, something you could wear to a cafe for a weekend brunch. Now that I was a racer, custom dictated that I couldn't look like one unless I was racing. Before, it had been fun to dress up as the real thing for rides like this. I suppose if you didn't know what to look for, I appeared to be overly thin, too clueless to wear padded shorts, and too cheap to buy a sophisticated bike.

"Catch them!" Natalie shouted.

"Let them go, Nut," I said. "You win a race with the last pedal stroke, not the first." We soft-pedaled as our little pack ping-ponged around us before bouncing away to chase the two eight-year-olds who'd gapped the group. Soon the road was clear ahead, and Natalie and I settled into a nice, steady rhythm, 70 percent of my max heart rate, 90 rpm. I could feel Natalie trying to match my cadence. We were doing maybe 17 mph.

I pointed out how green a green field was, and Natalie said hello to a sparrow eating a hot dog bun beside the road. We passed a crumpled, upright paper cup that, because of how its straw was sticking up, looked as if it were trying to hitch a ride. We passed a mother and a father, and a little girl on a shiny green bike. I said hello.

And that was the start of the string we reeled in over the next mile, the whole group coming back to us easily and without effort: The parents hectoring their eight-year-olds, the old guy wheezing as if he were imitating me after a sprint lap, and finally the kid on the mountain bike, who we passed on a small rise. He was out of the saddle, hammering. Natalie and I chatted as we sailed by.

I couldn't help myself. After I knew we were out of earshot, I turned my head to Natalie and said, "We're in first." That thing flickered in her eyes, the quick bright something I loved. There was a little upcurl at each side of her mouth. Sarah Uhl and Bobby Lea.

This was how it might have felt to them, I realized. The separation between me and these riders was as wide as the gap from me to the real racers. We were all racing, the charity riders and me and Natalie, and me and the pros and champs and legends. But none of us were really in the same race. Everything about a race, from the effort to the possibility, was different for each of us. I thought of something I'd once been busting Steak for. Although he would never get up for a morning ride with me, he let it slip that he'd been up at 7 A.M. to go to a rummage sale with his wife. I'd made fun of him for the fact that a rummage sale was a better motivator than a bike ride. He boasted that they'd discovered a box of orange Melmac for $8.

"People don't know what they have," Steak had said. "I could flip that tonight on eBay for a hundred dollars."

The Animal already had 54 points. Natalie wanted to win an untimed charity ride. The guy on the mountain bike wanted to beat a mouthy five-year-old. I couldn't figure out who was sillier—the people who gave away hundred-dollar Melmac for $8, or the people who thought $8 Melmac was worth a hundred dollars. So I spun my pedals.

Our bikes sang off the pavement, rising and falling like a melody over the gentle hills picked specifically for the shortest, easiest route of the Dream Come True. The wind rushing over my face was a friend today. A flock of birds scattered across the sky in front of us, like someone spilling pepper on a blue tablecloth. The road dropped down and left, and there was a sudden, sickening, sharp tug backward on my bike.

It was as if a giant hand had reached out and grabbed my rear wheel. My bike seized and went into a skid. Under the scritching, I heard a deeper, lower *thrum* and I knew the tow-bike was skidding, too. My bike fishtailed and started to slide out from under me, but I snapped my hips hard and recentered it. The resistance that had frozen my wheel let go as long as a finger snap, then clutched me again with another vicious yank backward and I suddenly understood that Natalie's bike was somehow no longer rolling, and that my bike was skidding uncontrollably because it was dragging a 30-pound tow-bike and a 36-pound passenger.

I didn't know if Natalie's bike had tipped, had gotten jammed, had broken, had gotten a squirrel stuck in its spokes—anything was possible, as it was also possible that my daughter was being dragged over asphalt at 20 mph under a steel trap that weighed nearly as much as she did.

Maybe two seconds had passed. Maybe one. My bike began writhing like a cut worm, and shuddering, and I knew we were going down. I horsed it back under me by driving my weight straight through my legs into the ground and lifting my forearms to pop the front wheel up away from the road to give it a chance to regain its inherent stability. As I did all that, I looked back and saw Nat hanging off the side of her bike.

Her face was terror, pain, disbelief. I couldn't see what was wrong, but her bike was upright and she was, so far, not dragging down on the road. I grabbed so much front brake the rear of my bike heaved, even with the weight of Nat's bike on it, and then I let off the brake and nailed it again, trying to slow us as quickly as I could without hurling Natalie off her bike, and I released the lever and flattened it against the handlebar, and we stopped.

I was off my bike. I held it with one hand to keep it from falling over and pulling the tow-bike down with it, and I began moving back to Nat. She had not yelled or screamed yet.

There was nothing in my sight but her face, her pain. I plucked her from her saddle, wrapping my left arm around her waist and lifting her, and she was screaming. An enormous patch on the underside of her right thigh, from the back of her knee nearly to her butt, was raw. Another, slimmer but just as long, stretched in a red jag from the front of her knee down her shin. She'd somehow slipped and gotten her leg caught between the wheel and bike frame.

The grated sections of her leg were already oozing translucent fluid, pink and orange. Black rubber from the tire had been friction-burnt into the edges. She screamed and shut her eyes with every breath, opened her eyes each time she gulped for air, and with them begged me to make this never have happened.

I hugged her to me and stroked her hair. I moved my hand down and manipulated her leg to bend at the knee, making sure nothing was broken or wrenched apart, and she wailed against my shoulder, shook. I stroked her hair and said, "Shhhhhh. Shhhhhhh. Shhhhhh. We can fix this. We can fix this."

"We have to fix this," said my father.

The bleeding had stopped, and he was frowning, scrutinizing the slit at the top of my nose. He was bent forward and leaning down, and I thought it odd that he'd dropped his head so low he had to roll his eyes up to look at me. I wondered why he didn't just bring his head level with mine. I supposed that, like the designated broken-nose washrag, this was the official broken-nose diagnosis stance. It did look somehow medical and learned, and in some way it comforted me.

"Stop crying," he said. I bit my cheek and held my breath and swallowed my sobs, but water still ran from my eyes.

"Stop crying." It was not a command, not a plea. It was some kind of statement of fact: I could stop crying, and should.

I chuffed once more and reached a hand up and wiped snot from my knuckles to my wrist. I blinked twice and stopped crying. My father put his hands on either side of my nose and rocked it back and forth. I could feel the top jiggling inside, sharp slices of pain.

"We could reset it," my father said. I didn't know what that meant. "But it doesn't look too bad. Do you want to leave it?"

I shrugged. I didn't know what we were leaving.

"We should leave it." He left the bathroom and I heard him rummaging around in his bedroom closet on the other side of the wall. I turned and looked at myself in the mirror over our sink. There was a red slash. No swelling. He was right: It didn't look too bad. But it hurt bad. Long, expanding throbs pulsed out from the inside of my head through the gap.

My father came back in the bathroom. He said, "We don't want to get into trouble," and lifted his right hand and showed me what he'd retrieved: a Cincinnati Reds cap. It was one of our family artifacts, supposedly an authentic one that his friend, Charlie Mexico, had snatched off the head of a player when we'd all gone up to Wrigley Field to watch the Big Red Machine beat the Cubs. I wasn't allowed to touch it, let alone wear it.

He plopped it onto my head, cocked up so he could see my face. "If we get into trouble," he said, "the whole family would fall apart. If I had to leave, none of us could stay to-gether. You don't want to cause that, do you? You don't want to be responsible for that."

He bent down again, but this time his eyes were level with mine, man to man instead of doctor to patient. His eyes drilled into me. "If you don't want to break the family up," he said, "you have to figure out a way to get your sister to hit you with the hammer when she and your mother get home."

The pounding waves redirected themselves, no longer pouring out of me but rolling from my nose back into my head to beat at my skull from the inside.

"She won't get into real trouble," my father said. "Not trouble that would make her leave and break up our whole family, like I'd have to leave if people thought I did it."

My skull started to come apart. I could feel a piece in back lifting away.

"Right?" my father said. He had my shoulders in his hands, jogged me and redirected the pain again, pivoted it back outward through the hole in my head, and it was just plain pain again, just ordinary hurt, and I nodded.

He pulled the bill of the cap down low over my face and lifted me off the sink and set me down and slapped my butt to send me off to play.

"Stop crying," I said to Nat. It was not a command or a plea. It was nothing, and she kept crying. Her leg convulsed. Her arms around me trembled. The shoulder of my jersey soaked through with tears and snot.

The kid on the mountain bike rode by us. Nat sensed his passing, or felt the shift in my muscles as I turned my head to watch him. She raised her face up out of the valley of my collarbone and stopped screaming. She snuffled. The old guy huffed past, bent over his handlebar.

91

I tipped Natalie back and kissed her forehead and her nose, wiped her cheeks dry with the hem of my jersey, wiped her nose then wiped it again immediately when more snot flowed out. Her blue eyes were just a hand's depth from mine. There was a tiny scar just below her right eye, from when she'd fallen and cut her cheek on a table a couple of years ago while running to get yogurt. At the emergency room, while admitting and treating her, the staff had probed creatively several times for the cause of the injury: "Has Daddy been bopping you again, sweetheart?" one nurse asked Natalie in a singsong. The process was calibrated to equally be considered insulting or easy to overlook; I remember feeling neither thing. I was grateful that they'd ask.

I held Natalie with my left arm around her waist and reached my right arm across her body, between us, and stroked the short length of her scar with the flat face of the nail of my index finger.

"Remember this?" I asked.

She nodded her head, snuffled up some snot, reached up with her fist, and cleared her nose. Her lips quivered.

"We made it all better, right?"

She nodded. "But it really hurts, Daddy."

"I know," I said, and I did. What cyclists call "road rash" is a common badge of the sport, seen throughout the season on riders' hips, butts, shoulders, elbows, forearms, and wrists. Because so many tiny nerve endings are exposed—the skin is the largest organ of the body—road rash is painful way out of proportion to its seriousness. It is, in fact, often a good sign. Grated skin means you didn't auger directly into the road, which concentrates the impact and is more likely to break bones.

It means you slid when you hit the pavement. Natalie had done essentially the same thing, though against the spinning tire. "I've wrecked and had boo-boos like that. I know it really, really hurts."

She lost some of her composure, blew a sob out of her mouth, and I tipped her chin up with my right hand and looked in her eyes again, level, father to daughter.

"But it is not at all dangerous," I said. "You are absolutely safe. It just hurts."

"It hurts a lot." She wailed again. I let her let it out, that pain in there, pulsing against her skin.

I had my mobile phone, but Beth was still out on her ride. The velodrome was a 20-minute drive for anyone I knew who could come to pick us up, and we were about four more miles from it. I knew a shortcut that could get us back in two.

"Listen, Nat," I said. "We have to ride back."

"No." It was a stretched, polysyllabic "no" that dropped down the scale and sat at Natalie's lowest note, vibrating. "Please. Please, Daddy."

"We have to ride, Boo. I can stop the hurting as soon as we get home and that's the quickest way home."

She wasn't getting on the bike.

I took my helmet off, then hers, and hung them by the straps over the handlebar of my bike and, still clasping her to me, I began walking. I noticed that her thigh was skinnier than my bicep. My feet crunched in the gravel beside the road. Nat made little involuntary sounds as my legs jogged her.

"*Phh, uphh, ahhh.*"

I walked. I thought it was strange that no other bikes had gone by.

"Daddy. My candy wrecked." She was pointing over my shoulder. I looked back. Her Mike & Ike boxes, bright green and purple, had been flung out onto the road. I dropped the bikes onto their sides and set Nat down. She stood on her good leg, dangling the hurt one with the toe just touching the ground, maybe a pose she'd learned in ballet class. I walked back and picked up the boxes, which were dented at the corners but intact. When I walked to the bikes, I counted. We'd gone seven steps.

I opened a box with my finger and squatted down and handed Natalie a candy and looked in her eyes. "We have to ride," I said, neither a plea nor a command. Just the truth. Natalie chewed the candy. She nodded.

In the end, it was easy. When Leann and my mother came home, I wheedled my sister out into the garage with the promise of breaking acorns on the hard floor with the hammer. The caps cracked crisply and neatly into pieces. The nuts squished, split, showed their sinuous insides.

"Lee-lee," I said. "Try hitting me with the hammer. Right here." I tipped back the baseball cap and pointed to the intersection of my nose and forehead, covering the red gash with my finger. "Let's see what happens."

And for some reason she did it. She could barely move the hammer, needed two hands to control it, and I'd figured there wouldn't be much of an impact. But as the heavy head crossed over the apex, Leann lost her ability to restrain the tool and it swung down with its full weight.

I screamed as if Leann had driven a spike through my head

and ran, first dripping blood, then streaking it, into the house, to my mother.

My father wasn't around. It was part of his genius that he always managed to vanish so completely from the aftermath of the chaos he created that you could never be sure he'd been there at all. Further, he was brilliant at composing explanations that not only obscured what had happened but covered reality under a thicker layer of artificial truth. It was a fact: Leann had hit me with a hammer.

My mother, who in all of our crazy situations was practical and forceful first, focusing on the actuality of what it would take to move ahead rather than on divining cause or effect, ran me to the kitchen sink on the end of her arm, pulled a dish-towel off a cabinet handle, and compressed it against my nose while soaking another under the faucet. In a few seconds she drilled the wet, cold towel against my face with her right hand, bracing her left hand behind my head for leverage. I had to push against the towel to keep my neck from being bent backward. The bleeding stopped in about two seconds, perhaps because my body made a systemic decision that if it didn't halt the blood its neck was going to be snapped.

My mother taped an X across my nose with white medical tape, gave me an ice pop, then asked me what happened and sent me back outside to play. She called Leann in as she ushered me out.

Later that evening, right before dinner, with a smeltering pot of pinto beans filling the house with a smell like cactus, fresh-cut wood and old clothes, my father, mother, sister, and I convened. My father was sitting on the couch. My sister and I stood next to each other in the arch between the dining room and living room. My mother commanded the center of the room.

"Show him what your sister did," she said.

I walked to my father, to his knees, which he opened so I could walk between them to get even closer. He peeled off one side of the X, left the tape flopping, then put his hands on either side of my nose, just below my eyes, and pulled down, gauging the wound as if it were a used car he wasn't sure he should buy. I could feel edges of the closed wound tearing apart.

"Damn," he said. He let my nose go and looked over at Leann, who was still standing under the arch. "Why'd you hit your brother with a hammer?" he asked. I could smell the sweetness of afternoon beer on his breath.

"He asked me to."

He looked at me. "That true?"

I nodded, and the whole incident became, in a way, my fault as well.

My father propped his head on one hand, fingers up on his forehead, thumb tucked under his cheekbone. He was looking at none of us, was staring down and away from all of us, seeing something we couldn't, distressed by our collective failure. "Would you do whatever someone asked?" he said. He raised his head and looked at Leann. "Would you hit yourself in the face with a hammer just because Billy asked you to?"

"No."

My father looked at my mother. "What kind of person does whatever someone else says to?" he asked.

It was likely that all three of us were playing roles of various importance in some grander drama only he could fully see. In addition to setting me up to frame Leann, he had probably prepped her for whatever she was supposed to contribute to this episode; perhaps when she'd first gotten home that day he'd somehow suggested that she hit me in the nose with a hammer, which would explain her rapid agreement when I mentioned it. (My sister and I talked once as adults about the incident, which she remembers being punished for but not perpetrating.) The inclusion of my mother might have been the endgame to something that had happened between them days ago, or it could have been groundwork he could refer back to in some future episode. What had seemed to me, as a kid, to be random bursts of anger were, as I realized as an adult, methodical and predatory. When my father set an incident in motion, the players might have, at best, a vague awareness of each other's participation but had to concentrate fully on their own well-being, as if we were all running atop a spinning log.

The actual breaking of the nose itself had been a mistake. My father rarely left behind physical evidence on me, or unexplainable remnants of his madness. Our dog—shot by a passing band of rogue kids with air guns. Broken chairs, soiled carpets, smashed toys—those were easily fitted into the province of childhood horseplay, mischief, and carelessness. My nose, it was apparent, had complicated things.

When he turned his face back to me, his eyes were hard. His breath washed over my face, up my cheeks, into my nostrils and eyes, into the new hole he'd put in my head. He said, "I mean, who the hell can you be if you do whatever someone tells you to?"

I carried Natalie into the house and put her on our bed, then went into the bathroom and got out the Second Skin, a wet bandage originally designed for burn victims that's great for road rash. Neosporin. Liquid soap. A washcloth. I carried Nat to the toilet and set her on the closed lid. I was going to have to scrub the rubber out of her raw skin. This was the worst part of road rash, so painful few people can do it thoroughly enough on their own.

"Boo," I said. "I am very sorry. This is going to hurt. But I have to do it."

"A lot?"

"I'm sorry. Yes. A lot. But it will be over quick."

I saturated the rag with warm water, dribbled some liquid soap onto it, and held it lightly against the road rash. Just getting it wet stings horribly, and Natalie shrieked and jerked her leg away, and I followed her with the rag, then began scrubbing.

She filled the house with her pain and during the worst of the scrubbing, she heartbreakingly tried to simultaneously run away from me and hug me, clutching me and repelling me.

When it was over, I lay her on the bed. She was breathing as if she'd been yanked from a drowning, not crying or sobbing, but whimpering. I covered most of her leg with Second Skin, smoothed gauze over that, and taped the edges.

Natalie said, "Daddy. It's okay."

"Yeah," I said. "It already feels better, huh?"

"No—it's okay that we didn't win. You're going to get ten points anyway."

I propped her up on two pillows, turned the television to cartoons, and went to the kitchen to retrieve a tray of macaroni and cheese, apple juice, and Children's Motrin. We cuddled on the bed and waited for Beth to come home. We'd each called her cell phone from the car, Nat leaving the first message: "Mommy. My leg got stuck in the wheel and I'm okay."

Over the years, I'd made up various stories about the sunken scar atop my nose. I told my wife and friends that Bobby Ferrell had kicked me in the face during a fight when we were kids, which he had. To the optometrist's assistant who was helping me pick out glasses and noticed that no frame would sit straight on my face, I turned the story about the time my sister conked me with a hammer into a comic caper. Sometimes I even made up stories for myself when I was out for a long ride, just me and the bike and the road for hours. I'd imagine that the thing my father and I were working on out in the garage that day was a bicycle, the sparkling blue Schwinn I learned to ride on. I have no idea if that's true, but I want it to be.

When bedtime came, Beth and I lay with Natalie, who had her injured leg propped up on a pillow, and we told her how brave she'd been. Then Beth turned out the light and left, and Natalie and I lay there while she told me stories. She'd developed one of those intense, ephemeral interests kids get, this time about Care Bears, and she was explaining the origins of each character for me. I kept losing the thread, because after my eyes adjusted to see by the glow of her nightlight, I was studying her face, thinking about something that happened that day during the awful ride back to the car. At one point I'd glanced back to check on her, and the rubble of her face—the wet and dried snot, the tear tracks turned pink by wind—had taken on a kind of nobility. Something about the line of her jaw, the tilt of her head, evoked not mere survival, not mere stoicism, but a pleasure in her survival, an unconsciously joyful recognition of her stoicism. Her five-year-old face had the complexity, and beauty, of a Roman ruin. I'd been so surprised, proud, puzzled, and even scared, in a way, to see such a thing in her that I'd stared back at her for too long and we'd run off the road into the gravel on the shoulder before I snapped my head back around and guided the bike onto pavement. I could find no trace of that in her as we lay there in bed.

"Daddy." She popped my shoulder to get my attention. "Tell me your favorite."

"Sure—what's yours?"

"Tender Heart. With the heart on his belly."

"Which one has the rain cloud on his stomach?"

"Grumpy Bear. You don't want him." Cheer Bear had a rainbow on his belly. Wish Bear had stars. She reviewed six or seven more. I liked several of them, but because I wanted to hear her talk, I didn't name a favorite. It was way past her bedtime. The moment for me to leave stretched out, got so thin it became transparent, then disappeared.

"I forgot Secret Bear," she said.

"That has some interest for me. What's on his belly?"

"Locked heart."

"I like him," I said. "Secret Bear. He's my favorite."

Natalie hugged me, and in the day's wash of warmth and love and worry, relief and regret, Secret Bear gave me the answer to my quest. He was stuffed, but his revelation for me was real. That damn bear told the entire world, anyone who cared to look, that there was something he could never tell them. He kept the secret itself hidden; but he used its power.

nine

THE LAST LAP WAS A WHOLE DIFFERENT RACE, A RACE within the race that I never dreamed existed. Ten of us were strangling each other at the front, a throat swallowing its own tongue, our walls constricting ever tighter inward. Handlebars overlapped, one in front of the other behind the next that was in front of the one in front of another, the clicking of them like a drumroll. The front of my pedal stroke spun inside the revolution of another racer's backward stroke, so that if one of us varied our cadence, our feet would collide.

The ten of us had dropped eighty-four riders. Among them: Steak. Swerve. Liz Reap, a friend of ours who would go on a few months later to win an amateur world championship on the track, and who, since she had abandoned the race, had been standing beside the course saying, "Patience," as I reeled by each lap.

I snorted and nodded to her each time. It was as if she knew

I was waiting for the perfect moment to release my rage. I could think of nothing more dangerous. Everything I'd achieved in my life, all that I was, had come from controlling the chaos that could erupt from inside me. Yet I needed that power to score ten points.

The ten of us were jigsawed together at 35 per, not one of us able to ride away, all of us waiting for the others to crack from the combination of speed and pressure, to crumble under the vise we'd constructed of our own effort and nerve. I'd gone this fast on a bike before and I'd ridden this close, but I'd never ridden this fast this close.

There was a bump from the back that became a slow, inexorable push, just the right move to make, the racers at the rear starting to go ever so slightly faster than those ahead, grandmasters choking each other to death with pawns. Sensing some barometric disturbance, some change in the pitch of the tone of the spinning gears, the riders bordering each side compacted inward.

There was nowhere to go. It was the finish. We closed on each other, shoulders skewed, bars and pedals and wheels buried in collapsed holes, hurtling along still at 35, and I swallowed my breath and held it until I burned, ten pedal strokes, five seconds. I exhaled.

I was supposed to win. I'd been a sure thing to win the sixthgrade spelling bee. I'd won every year since second grade. So, when I was eleven, my father studied with me for months, an hour or two a night, me sitting on the living room floor with my knees drawn up to my chest or lying flat on my back and picturing the words on the ceiling, him lying back on the big, overstuffed, tan and curvy mod chair that was wildly out of place in our traditional living room and reading off words from a mimeographed sheet my teacher had given me. My father missed his bowling nights to quiz me. He missed his favorite TV shows. Sometimes he and I ate dinner while he read off words. I knew *pusillanimous*. I knew *hagiography*. I knew *acetylsalicylic acid*, which I was pretty sure wasn't going to be asked because it was two words, but I lost that argument with my father and memorized it anyway.

I didn't know *corrode*, the easy word I drew in the second round of the bee.

We'd already planned a celebratory dinner at the Bonanza Steakhouse. Leann and I loved the thick slices of toasted yellow bread that disappeared in your mouth like cotton candy, and the spectacle of the high-flaming grills out in the open for customers to see. But in the parking lot of the elementary school, my father somehow changed our plans so Leann and my mother would go to dinner, while he and I drove home in his car. It felt normal, which was one of his gifts, the ability to wrap a blindfold of silky, soft lies and near-truths and inventions so gently over your eyes that it felt more comfortable than the strain of actually seeing.

When he and I pulled into the driveway, one of our babysitters was waiting outside the front door. Her appearance seemed even odder than the way our family had split up for the evening, but life with my father was always a fantastic conglomeration of improbabilities that resolved into a natural order. I went into my bedroom, alone, and began playing with a vast and motley collection of maimed G.I. Joes. After a while, my father called to me. I opened my door, took two steps, and froze.

My father was in the hall. His pants were down but not off, and he was shuffling toward me. His penis was wet. It was limp. It was uncircumcised, and it didn't look like a penis to me because there was no head. It looked like a rope. I could smell it.

He put his arm around me, and we shuffled into the living room together.

The babysitter lay submerged in my father's big, wavy chair, the whiteness of her skin breaking across the troughs of the chair's undulations from where we stood. As we shuffled closer I could see more of her: red hair, swollen lips, oval eyes. Her pastel pants lay on the floor like a melting swirl of mint ice cream. A light purple sweater was pulled up above her belly button and rumpled around to show one of her breasts, the size of my fist. She was smiling. There were wet marks on her, too, shiny transparent ones, and thick, white glops, and her red pubic hair was crazed, like a crayon picture of a fire, and the lips of her vagina were splayed open.

She liked to play Yahtzee. She made big bowls of peanut butter and jelly swirled together that she, Leann, and I ate with a shared spoon. She'd smooched me on the neck once. I'd drenched one of her boyfriends with the garden hose.

"Go on, son," said my father, giving me a push between my shoulders. The babysitter drew her lips back and away from her teeth. Without actually raising her ass, she moved it up and down, up and down, a slithery movement that seemed somehow as wet as the splotches on her skin. She smelled like a banana gone black.

My father reached down and unzipped the dress pants I'd worn on stage at the spelling bee. He stripped them down my legs to my ankles and pushed me hard toward the chair. "Go on," he said. "This is how my father taught me to be a Strickland."

I was up between her legs, and hard and scared and lost deep in her eyes no matter how much I tried to look away. No matter how much she looked away. Her hands fluttered down my back then swallowed my penis, and pulled me to her, and I felt one of my father's hands on my ass, pushing me to her.

It was molten.

I was away from her and out from under my father and scampering for my room, falling once in a tangle with my pants, but shucking them off and rising before the searing liquid smell of her could drown me. Back in my room, eventually I made two G.I. Joes missing their arms and legs battle to their simultaneous imaginary deaths.

She never babysat for us again. My father and I never spoke of her, or of what had happened. He just opened the door to my room the next night while I was playing. With one hand, he twirled the snub-nosed revolver he called a Saturday Night Special, the one he kept hidden in his bedroom closet where we all knew it was. He said, "You know I love you."

I nodded yes.

"And you know I'm also not afraid to blow your fucking brains out."

I nodded yes.

* * *

With a scorched, strangling growl, I stabbed my rear wheel hard left. It wasn't a change of line, or pressure fighting pressure, or any of the other moves that are considered hard but clean. It was a slash of pure violence, too quick to be seen.

Behind me, I heard cries: "Ahhh! Ohhh!" The pressure began to peel off our backs, then suddenly was sucked away. A vacuum had been turned on.

I heard metal tangle with metal, then shriek against asphalt. Someone yelped, "Yiiii."

At the corner of my vision, I saw feet at eye level. They rotated forward and down, and a bike appeared—crazy, out of place—from high in the air, upside down, whirling end over end, the rear wheel somersaulting by, then the front.

I'd forgotten it felt like this.

Over the gears, over the wails of our own hot breaths and under the deep rumble of my own joyous wrath, I heard human bodies hit the earth.

ten

THREE YEARS EARLIER, ON A WEDNESDAY MORNING IN October, I turned off my truck but left the keys in the ignition, inched open the door, and slid through the opening, then eased it back into the latch. I bent at the waist, holding onto the truck bed with one hand for support. After a while I squatted, then dropped to my knees, then onto my hands and knees as a spell of stringy spit heaves possessed me. When that was done, I got up and snuck into my home.

I opened and closed the back porch door with the same stealth I'd used on the truck, just in case Beth wasn't at work. But the house was aggressively empty, as if emptiness were not a state of being but a force, like gravity. I went into Natalie's room, kneeling beside her bed, which at that time was a miniature version of a princess bed, sized just right for her three-year-old body. I clutched her bedsheet, full of colorful kittens, in my left hand, and I pressed my face into her pillow, also populated with a rainbow litter of cats. I was losing my right to be in this room, smelling this pillow. I was losing my wife, my daughter, my job. I breathed in all that I could of Natalie, then I did not so much cry as split apart. I wasn't racked with great, heaving sobs. I simply opened up and began draining away.

The first time I laid my palm on Ruth's back and slid it along the expanse of her skin, I knew I could disappear into the broadness of her, in the valleys and mountains of the muscles of her body. She was nearly my size and weight, but opened in such a way that all other physical aspects of her—black, curly hair, and canine teeth that showed when she laughed, and all the rest—disappeared under her suggestion of borderlessness. She was a place the feral part of me could roam.

We'd known each other for less than a year. She was the marketing director for a company that worked closely with mine, her first office job after retiring as a cross-country ski racer. She'd been one of the best skiers in the world, relying on closing speed, but also an animal comprehension of weakness and opportunity. I'd always thought I could see in the way that she walked, or in how she rose from a chair or rolled her eyes at a meeting, that she'd become accustomed not merely to winning, but to defeating people. She was a predator trying to tame herself, and I found that intriguing.

Like all of us, I'd found people besides my spouse interesting, and attractive, and sometimes available. But the stakes had always been too high for me. I lived each day, sometimes each waking hour of each day, with the fear and full understanding that any crime I contemplated, from stealing a pencil at work to touching Ruth on the neck, could be the one that would trip whatever switch had so far held shut the door of my own cage.

There is no shortage of psychobabble explanations for why, one night in Ruth's car, I trailed a finger along her nape, then kissed her, then began a three-month affair. Beth and I had been pummeled by stress and the predictable trouble spots for a couple of years—the normal struggle to incorporate our first child into our marriage, promotions in both of our jobs, moving to a new home. We'd been through that miscarriage. Her father had died a few months before Nat was born. We'd been together, on and off, for nearly twenty years and married for nine. We were both just a few years shy of forty. But the simplest reason I betrayed my wife is the only one that ever mattered to me: My willpower failed.

I initially thought of Ruth as a kind of refuge for my worst impulses—a safe place to let myself howl. But I hadn't counted on the insatiable appetite of the awful part of me, which gorged itself on a desire that had little to do with romantic love or sexual lust. It felt as if I could finally breathe, as if I'd been pulled from something and smacked and had opened my mouth and blown out mucus and was sucking huge, fresh, bracing gulps of air, or as if I'd been swimming, swimming, swimming upward from a deep hole and had finally burst through the surface. The release was intoxicating, energizing, orgasmic, and never enough. You always want another breath.

I hated that I loved what I was doing. Beth, who for months had been warily observing the changes in my personality— "you're swaggering," she said to me one day, "you don't swagger"—began to openly question my fidelity. I lied. I smirked. I grew more reckless and more depraved. At my most repugnant moment, I canceled a shopping date with Beth; while she bought balloons for Natalie's birthday party, I snuck out with Ruth.

One night, inevitably, Ruth's husband discovered some e-mails she'd written to a friend describing our affair. When he called our house, Beth and I were putting Natalie down for the night. We were both kneeling beside her princess bed, a night light on, stuffed cats curled at her feet. I was singing "You Are My Sunshine," as the phone rang over and over; four rings, then to voicemail; then four rings again before a pause and four more rings.

"Get that," Beth called out to our niece Carleigh, who'd driven out from Indiana that weekend to visit her aunt, and was clearing the dishes from our Chinese take-out dinner.

I warbled, "You'll never know, dear . . ."

Carleigh walked into the doorway of Nat's room. Her face was scrunched. She said, "That was someone called Jimmy. He says he's—he says he's coming over to kick Bill's ass?"

I kissed Natalie on the forehead. She closed her eyes and I realized what I'd done.

I'd brought my father into my home. Into Natalie's bedroom.

When I was standing in our bedroom pulling on my shoes, Beth came in and said, "I know who that was."

"You do," I said. "It's Ruth's husband, and he thinks the same thing you do—that I'm having an affair with her."

"You are," said Beth, but I was already walking down the hall and out to the front door to wait outside for Jimmy and the start of the end of the life I had so carefully created and protected.

When he'd left—after he'd punched me, broken my left eardrum, and disappeared down the long, dark drive—Beth came outside and we sat on the asphalt, across from each other. We could see the shapes of each other, but no details. I could see Beth shaking, but not crying.

"I'll leave," I said.

Beth whipped her head back and forth in a violent no, and said, "I need to know about it," and dropped her face onto her knees. I told her some things and lied about some things, and we said what people say to each other, the heart-wrenching truths about disbelief, and agony, and broken trust, and through it all I knew there was only one solution.

"I need to leave," I said again after a while, and when I said it that time I understood that it was what I'd wanted all along, but had been too weak to do. I'd been counting on Beth to be strong enough to separate me from Natalie and go on to give our daughter the life she could never have around me. What I hadn't counted on was that Beth was even stronger than that.

"You need to stay," she said. "You're a bastard. You're a liar. You disgust me. I can't stand to see you or hear you or know you exist right now. But you're staying."

Though her family's spread had long since been bankrupted and split apart, my wife had never really stopped being the person who wrested a stuck calf from its mother's womb with a length of chain, who learned to drive a tractor when she was eight to spell her father during the busiest parts of the planting and harvest seasons, who got up at 3 A.M. to chase the herd back through the busted fence. With her father, she planted, harvested, planted again. They nurtured, they slaughtered, then they nurtured the next generation for slaughter. Floods came.

Droughts. Viral epidemics. They didn't wait for a new day to dawn; they got up before sunrise and ran the farm.

Beth and I went into our home, into our bedroom, and I asked if I should sleep in the basement.

"No," Beth said. "You sleep here. I'm sleeping on Natalie's floor."

When I met her in 1985, Beth was a girl, and even though I witnessed her transition into a wife and a mother, my dominant perception of her remained unchanged from the day we had met. I loved the woman, but fell in love with the girl inside the woman. That night, someone older stared out at me from behind her eyes. That woman in there pitied me, hated me, loved me, deliberately made me see her existence, and told me I could no longer have her, but also implored me to stay. I did not know what to do, what to say, how to stand or sit or move in front of that forbidding, sexy, tragic, unreachable woman. It was my habit to end each day by kissing Beth's mouth, then the tip of her nose, her forehead, and each closed eye. As we stood there, I made one lurching bend toward her mouth, and her eyes commanded me to stop. I did, and she leaned in and deflected her gaze and touched her lips to mine with a sorrowful linger, a kiss saying good-bye to something. She changed into pajamas behind her closed closet door and left the room. I took off my shoes but stayed dressed. I lay down on the bed. Sometime in the darkness, I left.

I drove the truck around for a few days, tried to sleep in the cab. I stayed in cheap motels, waiting to hear that I would be fired because my actions had compromised some of the contracts between my company and Ruth's. I tried not to remember my life as a father and husband, but would get stuck for hours thinking about a goofy ten seconds we'd all had together—the first time Natalie, practicing sentences, had told us, "I'll right be back," or when Beth had to admit to our doctor that she'd contracted her eye infection because we'd all made a game of letting Nat touch our eyeballs with her finger. I thought that if I could sneak back into what had been my home and say good-bye, I might be able to leave. I had to vanish. I could not do to my daughter what had been done to me.

After I left Nat's room and was sitting back out in the truck, I called Beth on my mobile phone. The connection clicked open. Neither of us said anything. The truck rumbled, ragged and shuddery. There was a hole in the exhaust pipe somewhere. I stared out the window at Natalie's sandbox. I'd let weeds grow up through it.

Beth said, "Without even a try?"

"I can't—"

"You're going to let this destroy us?"

The truck coughed, choked. The door rattled. A black bug crawled across the windshield.

Beth said, "Natalie needs us."

"She doesn't need this," I said, stabbing myself in the chest with a finger.

"No," said Beth. "This will destroy her."

"You have no idea," I said.

There was a pause full of digital crackling. Two seconds, maybe.

"You are a piece of shit," Beth said.

"You really have no idea," I said. "Can you save me?"

And Beth simply started us back to work. It was horrible

when I came home, of course—tense and too polite and all the things you hear reconciliations are. We went to therapy for a while; I told some funny stories about my father and my uncles and admitted to what the shrink called a life full of emotional noise, but I never said a word about the worst of it. Even so, the simple fact of having neutral ground to talk helped us. I lost the top spot at work, but kept my job. I romanced Beth. We went on larks, doing unplanned things like taking the day off work on a whim so we could drive down to Philadelphia to see Marcel Duchamp's bicycle wheel. We talked about us, but also about things like whether we believed in the universe or the multiverse, or whether we wished for Natalie a life of crunchy or smooth peanut butter. I made excuses to call Beth every time I went to the store for milk or to rent a movie, so she would know where I was. Somewhere in there Ruth was transferred to a division that didn't work with my company, then she moved out of town. I'd never talked to her again. Beth and I made a bunch of mistakes and wrong turns, and she slapped me once and beat me on the back with her fists, then cried and asked me to forgive her, which seemed ridiculous even to me, and that was really the point where the momentum of our lives pivoted and we knew we'd gotten around something.

And I rode. I rode more, and I rode often. I rode in the mornings at 5 A.M., and at lunch, and sometimes at night, down in my basement, my bike gripped by a stationary trainer that provided more resistance than real pavement. I rode before sunrise, with a light strapped to my handlebar, and I rode sometimes 300 or 400 miles a week, and I rode, and I got happier, and fitter, and I rode more. Beth forgave me a little, enough, and I rode and I was a good father. The awful part of me lay down and slept, so I rode some more to keep it sleeping—but what kind of life is that? What would happen when I stopped riding? I couldn't answer those questions. But I could ride my bike. So I rode my bike.

We got through two years like that.

In the middle of the cycling season in 2003, fitter than I'd ever been in my life, still scared, still desperate, I showed up for my first Thursday Night Crit. From that initial race, I discovered that—maybe because of my need to ride myself into submission, or my affinity for suffering, or my two decades of road savvy—I had a knack for riding beyond my physical ability, for sneaking into those select groups that shattered the pack. I inevitably got dropped within a lap of making those bold moves, but for a few minutes, I could ride among the best. Late in the season, I didn't get dropped. I hung onto a tiny pack and finished fourth in a sprint lap, and scored a point.

One point. The other names on the leader board, those above me, were cyclists who scored five, ten, thirty points a race, a hundred points or more a year. They were bike riders who won races all around the world, who were known and sometimes revered by cycling cognoscenti. Below me, not even on the board, were all the people like me—the fifty, seventy, hundred ordinary riders a week who tied themselves to that knot of suffering race after race, season after season, with no hope of ever scoring, setting their sights on the immense victory of simply being able to hang on.

That night, as Beth and I toasted my point with wine and gentle deprecation, I tried to explain both the accomplishment and the divide to Natalie. She looked at me and said, "Daddy. Next year you'll score ten points."

Ten points. That was out of the question, as impossible as becoming a father who not only never laid a finger on his child but who, in fact, never had to use the lack of child abuse as the measuring stick of good fatherhood. That was as inconceivable as being the kind of dad who judged success by what to others would seem to be the most mundane accomplishments: reliably contributing to a college fund or attending every ballet recital.

Ten points. Unimaginable. So I immediately promised Natalie that I would do it.

And my quest had begun.

eleven

As we pulled out of the parking lot after the crash-marred Crit, Nat reached around and opened the sliding windows that look back on the bed of the truck, where my LOOK was clamped into the rack.

"Your bike's sweaty," she said. "Can I open my window?"

"Bikes don't sweat," I said. My mouth was dry. My lips stuck together.

"Imaginary sweat. I want to open my window."

Beth and Natalie, who'd driven out, and Steak and Swerve and Liz, who'd all stuck around to see how I ended up, had been standing just past the finish line when I rolled across behind the lead group of five. I'd pulled over to them and braked and clicked out right away, instead of continuing on with everyone else for a cool-down lap.

"Let's get out of here," I said. I was trembling.

"Fast lap," said Steak.

"Bill!" said Swerve. "Did you see that wreck in the last lap?"

I shook my head.

"Like four guys went down! Endo!"

"It was behind me," I said.

"It was bad! So bad!" said Swerve, shrill and nearly shouting. His tone was a mix of terror and awe, as if he were a teenager who'd seen a car accident that exposed a beautiful woman's breast.

"Come on," I said to Beth and Nat. Before the race, Natalie had told me she wanted to drive home with me because she liked sitting up high, in the front and only seat, rather than in the backseat of our wagon.

Sitting in the truck now, even though I knew the evening air would be too sharp for Natalie's tiny body—and for mine, as well, which was sopping with sweat, partly because I hadn't even stopped to strip my jersey off—I said, "Go ahead, open your window."

"Okay. But I can't."

The truck didn't have power windows. I idled at the exit of the parking lot, reached across, and cranked the lever counterclockwise. The small effort made my body feel ashy. I rolled my window down, too.

Natalie stuck her face out the window, then pulled it back in. She said, "I need to tell you a joke."

"That's lucky," I said. "I really need to hear one."

"Knock-knock."

"Who's there?" I asked.

"It's not."

"It's not who?"

"It's not a pancake."

I erupted. I laughed and laughed and laughed, and Natalie curled up her mouth and looked proud. At a busy stoplight outside of the race course, a family in the car next to us looked up into the truck and said something about me. I began snorting out laughs then, chest-clenching explosions that pitched my head forward. Natalie began laughing at me laughing. She has a deep, rolling giggle that shows her miniature teeth and opens her mouth so wide you can see her throat, but her laughter is mostly in her eyes, like sparklers held aloft against a blue sky. Her surrender to silliness took me into one of those continuous, tremolo giggles that rose and fell depending on whether I was inhaling or exhaling, and as I looked to see if the light was green, I realized I'd been laughing so hard and long I was crying. I wiped my eyes, but made the mistake of shooting a look over to see if Nat's eyes were wet, too, and both of us spiraled off into wilder fits. Then somewhere in there I was crying for real.

I tried to make laughing sounds so Natalie might not know I was weeping. I sniffled, reached across the bench seat to Natalie, strapped up safe in her booster, and I cupped the back of her head in my hand then leaned over and kissed the top of her scalp. I said, "I'm glad you're not a pancake."

"Me too. Daddy, what are you not?"

I looked at her for what might have been infinity. A car behind us honked. What was I? What was I not?

"I'm not hot anymore," I said. While the car behind us honked and honked, I rolled up our windows.

twelve

ALARIC HAD SCARED NATALIE SILENT, THE CLOSE smelly warmth of his hospice room, the long, curving scar along the left side of his shaved head and his lolling, bloated face and listless, pale, swollen hands, and the animal grunts that had become his sole means of speaking.

I hadn't known it would be like that. When Natalie had heard Beth and me talking about going to visit Alaric at the hospice and asked to go along, Beth had flashed a look at me and said, "I don't know. He's really sick, Nat." But I had stupidly pictured some kind of movie scene: Alaric would lift Natalie giggling above his head, then toss her about like an uncle before sending her off to the kitchen for an ice cream while he pulled me aside; and though he was less than ten years older than me, wiser than ever from his perch on the brink of death, he would unveil the secret I lacked to score ten points.

Just three days earlier, I had once again, for the second Crit in a row, turned myself into a raging beast to stay with the pack and avoid getting dropped. I hadn't caused a crash this time, but had ridden wild enough to. The anger and the longing I'd unleashed in the Crit two weeks ago had scared me so bad that I'd vowed that I wouldn't—and couldn't—pay such a price just to score a point. But when I'd lined up, the organizer, Chip, had announced a rule change that in a single sentence dismantled my resolve: Because the fields had become too large and erratic, any rider dropped by the pack could be demoted by the judges to the early race—the learner event for kids, absolute novices, and those not skilled enough to call themselves real racers yet. When a shrill pop of the whistle started the race, I'd jumped inside, smacked against my own skin, misstepped when I tried to click in, fallen to the back, and never really gotten into the heart of the pack. Failure no longer meant the mere lack of a point; it meant that everything—the season, the dream of scoring ten points, and the hope that those points could turn me into the most extraordinary thing of all, an ordinary father—would be dead. The decision to set loose the worst part of myself for the second week in a row had been easy, which in itself unnerved me.

So when Natalie had asked if she could visit Alaric with us, I'd said, "Sure. I want you to. If I know Alaric, he'll have something to tell you and me." But once we got there, it was instantly apparent that if Natalie retained any memory of the man, it would not be as the person he was to me.

Alaric's brother, who looked about my age, sat down on the bed and put a hand over one of the slight hillocks that were Alaric's legs. His mother sat on the other side of the bed, cajoling pudding into his mouth with a plastic spoon. His brother said, "So you're one of his riding friends?"

I shook my head and swallowed. Beth, who was standing beside me, put her hand on my shoulder. Natalie was behind us, pressing herself against the back of Beth's legs. "He was my coach," I said, and immediately regretted the past tense. "I mean, he's alive. Of course. I mean he coached me a long time ago. One summer."

At the last class of the summer, Alaric wanted us to try a race called the miss-and-out; at the end of each lap, the last person to cross the finish line is pulled from the track. There were seven pros and top-level amateurs doing some training there that day, and Alaric put them on the track with us to keep the speed high and smooth—safer.

"You'll kill your bloody selves, won't you, if I let you miss-and-out alone," he said.

One by one our class dropped out. On the ninth lap, I came around the gifted young Princess from two bike lengths back to put her out. On the tenth, I beat the ex-racer Suds by no more than the width of a tire. It was me and seven real racers circling the track. I would be the next one out.

I finished third.

I smiled, dying, all the way around my recovery lap, and when I got near the finish, Alaric gave a short wave of his arm. I rolled in his direction and he walked toward me. When I was near enough, he grabbed my shoulder and leaned in. He rested his forehead against mine and kind of rolled it back and forth, as if we were bears.

He whispered, but like his speaking voice, it was a big

whisper that filled the area bounded by our heads and arms. "I need you to think hard on something for me, Bill." He paused, and though not long, it, too, was big and heavy. "Why is it that you ride better when you're about to lose than when you're about to win?"

"Oooooh," said his mother. "So he made you into one of his racers."

"Well, no, I . . ." I looked at Alaric's eyes. "I never raced."

"Ah, but you look it," said his brother, appraising me. "Alaric, remember Daddy would always pull the skin on our thighs and say, 'Not enough miles?'"

Alaric gurgled into his food. His brother looked at me and explained, "If Daddy couldn't lift any skin off our legs he'd say we had enough miles. I'd say you have enough miles."

"Well, I . . ." I looked at Alaric's eyes. Then I looked into them. "I'm racing now, Alaric."

I took a step forward, then two more to get around Alaric's brother, and I walked up to the head of the bed. I looked back. Beth had unpeeled Natalie's arms, ushered her around Alaric's brother, and was kneeling beside her, whispering. Natalie was peering at Alaric and me.

I wanted to lean in and touch my forehead to Alaric's and roll against it as if we were comrades on a sunny summer Saturday morning, but I was afraid of what his family would think. I wanted to tell him that I had to score ten points to save my daughter from a curse so abhorrent I'd never told a single person about its existence, let alone its particulars. I wanted to tell him I was failing. I wanted to ask him if he thought there truly might be fates worse than dying. I wanted

to ask him if he was angered or amused by my selfishness. And
I wanted to ask him, please, could you tell me, because you
know everything about racing and more of life and death than
I do, could you tell me if using evil to destroy evil is the right
thing to do—because it feels like the only way I can succeed at
the same time that it feels terrifying and wrong. I wanted to ask
him: What should I do, Coach? Scream at me and I'll decipher
it this time, I swear. Should I go now? Go down? Not now?

I could already hear his answer reverberating in my head.

Why?

In the car as we drove home, Beth reached over from the passenger seat and turned up the radio so she could speak under
the music and not be heard by Natalie in the back. She said, "I
think it was good to bring her."

"Yeah?" I said. I shot a glance backward. Natalie hadn't
spoken since we'd gotten into the car.

"She won't remember it," Beth said, "but she'll always
know that she came to see him."

Natalie said something we couldn't hear over the music.
Beth twirled the dial down and said, "What'd you say, honey?"

Natalie said, "I hope he lives."

I took a long look over at Beth, who squeezed her eyes shut
while facing me, then opened them and turned toward Nat. I
tried to think of a way to tell our daughter that Alaric wasn't
going to live.

Natalie said, "I hope he lives—until it's time for him to die."

"I think it's time, sweetie," Beth said.

"I know," said Natalie. "Do you think his heart is as light as
a feather?"

"Alaric?" I said. "Oh yeah. No question." Hanging in the hallway to our bedrooms is a framed papyrus scroll that Beth and I bought in Egypt. In the pictograph, a long line of deceased wait for a chance to set their hearts on a scale that's balanced on the other side by a feather. Weigh out light, and you're rewarded with life everlasting. Tip heavy, and the crocodile god poised in the background eats you.

Nat said, "My heart is as light as a feather."

"Lighter, Nat," said Beth.

"Pure light," I said. A flash of Bobby Lea and Sarah Uhl smiling, of Natalie leading the Dream Come True ride.

Nat said, "So is Mommy's."

"Oh yeah," I said. "Even after dealing with me."

Beth jogged my shoulder and said, "Barely."

From the backseat, Natalie said, "Daddy, you better be making your heart light."

Beth laughed. I nodded.

Alaric died two days later. His funeral was the morning of the next Crit. Nearly a hundred cyclists showed up at the church on bikes and in full riding gear, click-clacked down the pews, sat through a sermon, then went outside to pay our respects to his wife and daughter. Three by three, in more than thirty rows, we pedaled along behind the hearse. Beth and Liz Reap and I were in a row. It was just a short three miles to the cemetery, but on the last little hill before the gate I looked back and saw that, even in this funeral procession, we'd dropped some of the group. I had to laugh.

Like all of the other Thursday Night racers who stood there in the cemetery grass, I wanted to score a point later that day to honor Alaric. I'd sharpened my fitness with 107 miles since I saw him alive, getting up at 4 A.M. and 5 A.M. to ride before work, and riding at lunch both days as well. I vowed to the dirt lying at my feet that I would do whatever it took on top of that to score a point, no matter how heavy it made my heart.

At 4 P.M., as if Alaric were booming out one of his directives, the sky went black, then split open, and the Crit was rained out.

thirteen

Just a few laps into the next Crit, it rained again, the first big drops smacking the asphalt with a sound like open-handed slaps.

I was at the front of the pack on Bird's wheel—Bird who was fast not like an eagle but like an emu. He was one of the rare racers who'd found a way to be successful even at six feet plus and two-hundred-something pounds. He moved as if not all of his parts were receiving instructions from his brain at the same speed, but thanks to sheer wattage and the laws of physics—once he got rolling he tended to not slow down—he was one of the best wheels to follow at the Crit.

Five or six guys had been taking turns trying to push me off Bird. Because of his volume and massive frontal area, the draft he gave was no mere blocking of the wind. It was almost a kind of sucking forward, a vacuum that helped pull you in tight behind him. Someone in red and white came up and laid his helmet against my shoulder and pushed sideways. I tried something I'd witnessed the Animal doing: Instead of pushing back, as you were expected to, I leaned away from the contact while keeping my bike centered under my hips and glued to Bird's wheel; then I reversed and pitched my torso against the unbalanced rider. He and his bike flew sideways, away from me and out into the wind. He hung there for a second or two, then vanished backward.

I was racing hard, but clean. That was the deal I'd made with myself when the Crit had been rained out on the day of Alaric's funeral. Natalie had a better chance at a normal life if I lost as myself than if I won as the thing I'd worked all my life to avoid becoming. In my desperation to do anything to be unlike my father, I'd been becoming him, acclimating myself to the worst part of who I was. I'd been teaching myself, as my father had said, to be a Strickland.

Rain thonked on my helmet. The drumming filled my head as if I were chewing food with my ears stopped up. As we passed the line with two laps to go for points, the rain stopped falling on us and erected itself in front of us, a new wall of stings we smashed through with every pedal stroke.

The pavement became slick. My rear wheel slid out from under me and I snapped my hips to bring the bike back beneath my body. The front wheel skated sideways, making a sound as if it were shushing a child and, without knowing how, I straightened it. As I pedaled into the corner before the hill, my whole bike drifted half a foot toward the outside of the turn. Panicked, I waited for the racers I must have cut off to scream at me. But there was only the bashing of the rain against my head. I looked back and there was no one with me.

I'd dropped the pack.

I tried to remember the last time I'd heard a bell or what number the lap counter had shown. I spun the pedals. I pulled the bike back under me again and again. I rode up the hill and down into the woods, and Bill Elliston came up beside me. His upright, relaxed riding style was like the absence of the idea that there should be riding styles. He rode as if there were only one way to ride. I was pedaling across the wet pavement as if I were trying on ice skates for the first time. But it was him and me, alone out front. Elliston had done pretty good against some of the gods of the European peloton at a big pro crit that had been run around Wall Street in Manhattan with tens of thousands of spectators on the sidewalks ringing cowbells and cheering. He looked over at me to see who I was—he didn't know me—and I shrugged. He regarded me from somewhere inside the implacable body that relaxed on a bicycle going 30 mph in a thunderstorm.

We crossed the line. There was no bell. The two officials were standing and waving wildly. For a mad second, I thought they were as overcome with emotion at my ride as I was. Then I heard the woman yelling, "Done!" The man picked up the lap counter. The wind tore a hole in the wall of rain and ripped the lap board from the man's arms, and the sky dropped on us. It was the kind of soaking where in two seconds my shoes were filled with water.

Elliston was sitting up and coasting and so, I realized, was I. The pack streamed around us and scattered for the parking lot.

I pulled over to the grass and unclipped. I took my helmet off and hung it across my stem and handlebar, so it aimed out from my bike like the sculpture on a ship's prow. I stood there getting drenched. Steak jogged over, abandoning the dubious cover of the tree that stood near the finish, hunched and holding his head in that futile ducking posture we all use in a downpour. I became aware that I was smiling, happy, loose.

Steak said, "What was that? You were killing those guys." He smiled. He put a hand to his forehead. He'd had a bad wreck a few days earlier on a metal-grate bridge, catching his thumb in one of the holes when he went down. One of his pedals had also gotten caught in the grating, and the force had been strong enough to bend the thick aluminum crankarm that held the pedal. Steak was lucky he still had a thumb. He said, "Maybe there's your secret."

"What?" I said. "Make it rain every Crit day and score a point before the race gets canceled?"

"Something like that. Let's get out of here."

I pedaled across the grass and Steak jogged beside me. As we crossed into the parking lot, Steak said, "What I meant was, figure out what made you so good in the rain and use that." He ran off toward his car. When he reached the door he gave me a wave, not waiting until he'd fully turned to do it, but starting the gesture as he turned, as if he were sure that I'd still be straddling my bicycle in the parking lot, letting the storm fall on me.

Unfortunately, the next Crit was as sunny and clear as you'd expect an early Thursday evening in late June to be, 89 degrees, nearly windless, the asphalt a deep, beautiful melting tarry black.

The pack had decided to liquefy itself. There were sixty of us bunched up so tight, so fast, that when one of us popped we didn't have room to explode or even gradually fray apart over the course of a mile. One by one, we were simply turning to fluid and streaming out the back of the thing we'd once been part of. No one attacked; there was no need to. At the end of this alchemization, the winners would be left.

About halfway through, as the summer humidity deepened, a steady, stinging rainstorm of sweat began flying backward through the pack, salty and heavy with electrolytes. Somewhere near the front, a guy in a yellow-and-black jersey turned his head and puked out a loogey that was spread and flattened into a kite by the turbulent swirl passing over the pack. It sailed over the field of bright helmets and spattered from jawline to eye onto the face of the guy in dead last—me.

I kept my hands on the bar and pedaled. I didn't have the time or energy to wipe away that or any of the other second-hand slime shellacking my body.

The bell rang for the last sprint, and the bobbing black butts and tan calves and white shoes in front of me receded. I was a wheel's length off the tail. I thought: *Knock-knock.*

Who's there?

I'm not.

I'm not who?

I'm not my father.

I ground my teeth and tasted something chalky, and snot and sweat and acid and vomit, and I screamed and I groaned and flailed into contact with the tail—and it was me doing it, not some dark part of me. I heard Natalie yell, "Dadda!" I was thirty-nine. I was wet with other people's waste, and sore not from this race but from a few hard laps on the wheel of Bill Elliston in the rain a week ago, and the pack stretched out the nothing between itself and me, and I closed my eyes and emptied myself of every human thing in my body, and mind, and of all thought, and of past and present, and then I got dropped.

On the way home in the truck, Natalie and I passed the Animal—who rode his bike to and from the race, just to get a better workout. Natalie leaned out her window and waved at him and said something I couldn't hear. She watched him fall away from us for a few blocks, then brought her head back in. She said, "He's gone."

Counting all the Crits I'd done, and the one that Alaric had rained out, there had been ten this season. Maybe each failure had been a point, part of a process that I'd needed to go through to understand that there were no magical solutions— that instead of erasing the possibility that I might enact my family curse, I needed to accept its existence and steel myself to battle it my whole life. And maybe that was what this had all been about.

My mind searched for some solution, anything to help salvage me, to keep me driving home and chatting with Natalie about topics like whether we could have a pet whale, and to keep the panic that was rising up through me from exploding.

Natalie looked at me and said, "Slow down." I yanked my foot off the gas pedal and looked at the speedometer to quantify how bad I should feel about scaring her. I'd only been going about twenty, neither too fast nor too slow for the traffic on this stoplit road. I looked over at Natalie. She had her head craned out the window, looking backward. I stared into the rearview mirror and saw Paul Pearson riding up the side of the road, getting closer.

Natalie pulled her head in and said, "Here comes the Animal, Daddy."

fourteen

I WAS NOT MY FATHER.

I knew that on the airplane to Phoenix, just three days after I got dropped in the Crit, when Natalie turned sideways in the seat she occupied between Beth and me, stared at me, and began clicking her teeth against each other, loudly and obviously chewing on nothing. I picked up the red milk carton sitting on the seat tray in front of her and, as if I were pitching something in a commercial, said, "No biting milk."

Once Natalie had become old enough to start creating her own mischief and peril, Beth and I had begun keeping track of the ridiculous pronouncements we heard each other improvise during the act of parenting. No hugging bread. No stuffing elephants up your nose. No wiping your plate with flamingoes. These, along with "no biting milk" and about twenty other pieces of wisdom, were written on a sheet of paper that was labeled "House Rules," and hung on our refrigerator door. Our list of odd aphorisms made me happy every time I noticed it. It was an affirmation of the hilarious chaos of raising a child, but it also seemed to be proof that Beth and I would do whatever it took to make the world safer and more sane for our daughter without regard for our own dignity. There it was in writing: I was the kind of father this funny, smart, curious daughter deserved. Over time, though Beth and I still remarked "House Rule" when one of us quashed a problem with some inane pronouncement, we rarely bothered to write the new ones down. We'd grown accustomed to the strange rituals required by parenting, and House Rules became just one more aspect of our lives together, as we no longer videotaped soccer practice, and sometimes took books or office work to occupy ourselves at Nat's swim class. What had been novelty became normal. For me, that was even better.

And there we were on the plane, just a regular family goofing off, sharing a private joke, getting away for a vacation together. When we'd first begun planning the week-long, guided camping trip at the Grand Canyon, nearly half a year ago, I'd caught myself selfishly resenting it because the vacation would cost me one Crit. Now it seemed perfect. I could take this time to accept that my quest for the magical ten points was over. I was sure that, in some way, the experience of failing to get ten points had given me some kind of knowledge I could use to become an ordinary dad, some insight I might fall back on in my darkest times, if only I could uncover it. I wanted to use our seven days away from civilization to figure out what edge I had gained. We were not a family that would face its travails without wisdom. As proof, in a slightly raised and stern voice, I reminded Natalie and

Beth that, according to the established rules of our family, on this trip there would be, "No announcing the number of flies in a restaurant."

I was not my father.

I had failed to get ten points, in plain sight and bare of mitigating context. I'd never seen my father fail at anything. If he couldn't get the vodka from the bottle, he'd lap it up from the ashtray. When he quit a job, he had triumphed over a power-mad tyrant. When he got fired, he had not backed down from those with more money and less principle. When we couldn't afford to buy the toy construction set that contained a crane I needed to complete my science project that demonstrated how a blast furnace worked, my father broke open the package and stuffed the crane up my parka, then made me walk out of the department store five minutes ahead of him—a victory for the small guy who shouldn't have to pay a multimillion-dollar corporation for an entire kit when all he wanted was one piece. When he faked the theft of the used Chevy Nova that started breaking down the day he bought it, setting it on fire in a sand pit to collect the insurance, he was a crusader for justice and fairness. Every disaster became a caper, every misstep an escapade.

Once when I was somewhere between three and seven years old, I'd been in the backseat of a big, loud, brown car my father and his brother, Gary, were taking turns driving. We'd walked to a bar from my grandmother's house and left in this car after examining several in the parking lot. Whichever brother was in the passenger seat would chug from a series of bottles they kept producing and dispatching out the windows.

The other would make the tires scream, and rip doughnuts across both lanes of a country road in West Virginia.

As my father was gunning the car through a long series of maneuvers that left smoke trailing behind us, a white blur shot up and over the rise of the road from the other direction, squealed its brakes so hard the sound was audible even over the internal roar of our car, and desperately dodged us, sliding to a long, screeching, gravel-throwing sideways stop in the dirt and brush of the shoulder. It was a cop car.

Gary's hand was clutching the dash. "Holy fucking mother, Billy Joe," he said. "You're in it now."

Our car had stopped, miraculously pointing straight down the road. It rumbled under us. My father punched the gas. We plunged down the curving road, along deep forest, beside dynamited rock, outrunning the sound of the siren that must have been pursuing us. We kept waiting to hear it. I kept a lookout for the whole squadron of police that was going to appear behind us, force us off the road, then ram us into one of the ravines my father kept skirting. Finally, at the bottom of a valley, my father looked in the empty rearview mirror, braked, and pulled to the side of the road. When we were stopped on the shoulder, he raised his arms as if he were stretching the fatigue out of his body after an all-night drive, sighed, then turned to Gary and said, "Brother, I'm a little tired. How about you drive for a while?"

He opened the door and stepped out, cool and casual, as if he really were merely trading seats for a nap. For whatever reason, no cop ever came, and I no longer remember if my father and his brother actually did swap driving duties. What stuck with me was the authentic transformation of a mistake into just one more rollicking tale.

I wanted to explain to Natalie that my chance to fulfill her dream was finished. I imagined that sometime during the week of our vacation, with the magnificence of the Grand Canyon as a reminder in contrast, I could find a way, stripped of color and dimension, to tell my daughter that I had failed.

I was not my father.

When our guides pitched camp near a fire tower and Natalie wanted to climb it, I went with her up the swaying skeletal metal stairs, coaxing her up the last ten steps and then up the ladder into the open trap door, where the odd lady at the top asked us to blow bubbles with her. We leaned out the window, 80 feet high, to watch the transparent spheres bounce along the wind currents over the trees. Natalie had never seen me helpless on the floor beneath her, drooling, convulsing. She had never seen me the way I'd seen my father.

His epilepsy nearly vanished at different times throughout his life—he claimed, in various degrees of stridency, that he'd medicated it with alcohol, banished it with willpower, turned it over to God, and that a mutt we owned had taken the illness into itself, for which he said there was medical precedent. When I was four or five, he suffered as many as five seizures a week. As I got older, I remember him having just one or two a year.

If he was walking when the epilepsy came upon him, he'd begin to stagger. If he was sitting, his head would bob, then fall to his chest as if he were nodding off. Thick, white, foamy drool would erupt from his mouth. His hands would clench into claws, and the seizing muscles in his neck would whip his head back as if he'd been struck from behind. He'd fall to the floor and begin hissing, choking, crying out long, ululating syllables that did not mix vowels and consonants.

I'd been tutored to stay away from his whipping limbs while clearing away any hard, sharp-edged furniture I could move. Then, even as a four-year-old, I would call the police—this was before 911. I had the seven-digit number and our address memorized. When I got a few years older, my mother taught me to crawl between his flailing arms until I could cradle his head in my knees and stick a cushioned tongue depressor into his mouth, which we believed would keep him from biting off his tongue.

If he was just having one seizure instead of a series, he would finish before the police and ambulance arrived. The seizure would diminish from wild swings to jerks to spasms to quivering, then to just sounds—gurgles and growls and even woofs, as if he were imitating a dreaming dog—and then nothing but a line of spittle running down his cheek, and whatever blood he'd drawn from his knuckles or elbow or forehead.

My father would open his eyes. He'd cast them at me in fear, confusion, unaware of where he was or who either of us was. Sometimes he would try to rise and run from me, but he was too weak to break my grasp. So he always lay there, head in my lap, searching my eyes until he remembered who we were, what had happened, and that he was helpless. That was when his eyes showed bottomless loss.

I was not my father.

People who had never known him told me that. One day our camping group—us, plus another family with two boys and a girl, all within a couple years of Nat's age—was scheduled to hike a short way down into the Canyon. We stopped first at the rim so the guide could give a talk about geology and history.

Natalie, Becca, Trent, and Bailey were far more interested in the cigarette bin near the rail, a treasure of crushed glass of brown, yellow, and green that sparkled and glittered in the summer sun. I was more interested in the kids who were interested in the cigarette bin. As the guide explained the geologic eras visible in the canyon walls, the kids punched each other, whispered, and were politely shushed by us. Eventually I raised my hand and said, "Um, Dee? If we're going to get anywhere, I think first you need to explain this garbage can to us."

The kids and Beth and I, and the other parents, Andy and Patty, and even Dee, laughed with relief as much as amusement. For about thirty seconds we focused our attention on an ash can at the edge of one of the world's natural wonders.

The steps set into the walls of the Canyon were chest-high to the kids, so we ended up only hiking down a quarter mile or so, a good hour's labor. On the way back up, Nat began to fatigue and asked if I'd carry her. It was so hot we'd all been guzzling water and were nearly out.

"I'll carry you," I said. "But if you make it to the top on your own, Mom and I will get you a special prize before we leave." That morning, we'd stopped to buy drinks in a gift shop she desperately wanted to revisit.

"You won't carry me?" Natalie whined.

"I will. But I think it'll mean something if you hike out yourself," I said.

Natalie was wearing Beth's baseball cap low over her eyes.

Her hair hung in sweaty strands alongside her cheeks. Both knees were skinned from scrabbling over the rocks. "I want you to carry me," she said.

"Okay," I said. I picked her up and held her against my chest. "You understand your choice, right?"

She kicked out of my grasp. "What will it mean if I walk?"

"I don't know," I said. "But it will mean something."

She sighed, exasperated with me. "It will mean I get a prize."

I heard one of the adults, Beth or Andy or Patty, snicker.

Nat made it to the top. As we rested up there, Patty, who was an elementary school teacher, said, "You're a good father. A natural."

I was flattered, embarrassed. I laughed out a short little breath, and said, "Oh, I could tell you stories."

Patty said, "We all could."

And for a moment I wanted to tell this stranger about the carnage inside me, not only what I had endured, but what I was capable of. I closed my eyes and lay down at the edge of a deep hole.

No, I was not my father, and so those unreachable ten points should not have mattered.

We were camped amid the scrub of the Kaibab Plateau, in the shadow of boulders as high and half as wide as our house. Becca, Bailey, Trent, and Natalie were scampering across the sand and high up onto the rocks to the farthest edges of our sightlines. They kept bringing for our inspection smooth pebbles, pieces of sun-washed wood, little bones, bugs on sticks. During one drop-off of booty, Natalie asked me for permission to take her sweaty shoes off and run barefoot through the sand and scrub.

"No way," I said. "You'll step on cactus, Boo."

"I won't," she said.

"No. Look—none of the other kids are barefoot."

"Daddy. I'll be careful." Her eyes became faintly lamb-like, wet. "Please?" she whispered, and ducked her head.

"It's not about being careful," I said.

"You never let me do anything." She kicked at the sand, spritzing some out onto a few of the camp chairs arranged for dinner.

"Fine," I said. "You take those shoes off. You go out and play. You are going to step on a cactus and it is going to hurt. Do you understand that? Do you understand the choice you are making?"

She nodded and stripped her shoes off and ran out across the sand to play.

I heard her screaming.

She was sitting, feet raised in the air, screeching and looking for me. I ran to her, scooped her up, and ran back to the van where one of the guides had the passenger door open and was getting out a medical kit.

"I'll do it," I said, and sat Nat sideways in the seat, her legs hanging out the open door. The soles of her feet were pincushioned with translucent slivers, no thicker than the fine hair on her head. Natalie screamed, yowled.

I held her shoulders and said, "Let's do three calming breaths," and we looked into each other's eyes and inhaled and exhaled three huge times.

She was crying, but quiet.

"I'm going to take them out now," I said, "and then it will be better." I took the tweezers from the guide and, as smoothly and softly as I could, I eased out the first needle.

"Are there a lot?" Natalie asked.

"Yeah."

She cried harder, but she did not scream. She said, "Why—why did you let me go barefoot? Why did you?"

"It's for your own good," I said. "It's for your own good."

fifteen

"IT'S FOR YOUR OWN GOOD," MY FATHER SAID, "YOU piece of shit."

Lying askew on the dinner plate on the table in front of me, there were two dry, flaking rolls about the size and shape of two of my fingers and a shade of gray closer to no color than any actual hue. There were washed-out, grassy strands woven throughout and sticking out here and there like whiskers, and there were flecks of dark yellow all around, and two or three sunken, bright white spatters that looked hard. They didn't smell. Even if they had reeked of what they were, in my home, on my dining room table, on a plate we used every day for meals, there was no sufficient context that would allow me continuous recognition. I kept disbelieving what they were.

"Eat them," my father said. He put one hand flat on the table in front of my plate and the other on the high back of the dining room chair I sat in, then leaned down and put his

143

mouth next to my left ear. His silver-rimmed glasses bumped the side of my head. Low and breathy, but not whispering, each word chopped off from the others, he said, "You. Fucking. Eat. Them."

I was in sixth grade and I'd had the bad luck to have done something, when my father and I were alone in the house, that had led to him sitting me down at the table to tell me that I was a piece of shit, that I wasn't worth shit, that I had shit for brains, and that I didn't know shit about shit. I was crying when he left, but it was stagy, and as I sat there and bawled I was already thinking about what TV shows I might watch later that afternoon. I heard the back door open, slam shut, open and slam again a minute or two later. A cupboard door banged open. Something clinked. My father came back into the room and flung a plate onto the table like an angry waiter.

Dogshit.

I turned and tipped my head up and looked up into my father's eyes. They were not pulsing and angry. They were bottomless, the infinite holes of loss. I picked up one of the turds with my thumb and index finger and brought it to my mouth and bit half of it off.

All my life I've wished that I had resisted, said no once, made him scream or hit me or smash my face into the plate, or at least threaten to, before I ate that first piece of shit.

It crumbled and became chewy and muddy in my mouth, like a cake mix made too thick. There were tiny, sharp hard pieces that hurt my gums, and grit that ground between my teeth. As it got wetter, the taste of it, the shit taste, rose up into my nose. My throat constricted. My head felt as if it were floating off my neck and my heart inflated in a single huge bass thump against my chest then seemed to seize three or more seconds before finishing the second, deflating half of its thundering beat. My tongue became a foreign thing in my mouth, as distasteful to me as the shit itself. My stomach clenched and my heart began punching itself out like a speed bag. My head grew hot and heavy, as if it were filling with lava. I gagged. Spittle and wet flecks of shit dribbled out onto my lower lip and chin. I swallowed what was left in my mouth. I wiped my chin and my father took the plate away.

"That's right," he said. He raised the plate and swept it outward, away from us, gesturing to all that was not us, and the two pieces left on the plate fell off and broke apart on the table. "You get used to swallowing shit. The whole world wants you to." He poked me in the chest with the plate. "You get used to that taste. It's for your own goddamn good."

sixteen

THE HOWLING PULLED ME UP OUT OF AN UNSTIRRING, undreaming sleep and, without awareness of the moments between, I was out of the tent where Beth and Natalie still lay. I was barefoot in the cool sand, soft and shifting beneath my soles. Sagebrush scratched my calves as I stumbled toward a small rise. I stopped on the high spot and turned my face up to the full, bright, white moon, feeling absurd and primal all at once, and I hung motionless, letting the two emotions fight their way through me until the ancient part of me won.

I raised my hands to the moon, a scrawny middle-aged man in striped designer briefs. I stretched my arms higher. Joints in my elbows popped. I raised onto my tiptoes, swaying for balance as I reached for the thing that draws our howls out of us.

The keening animal chorus soared and dipped, sometimes falling full and lush from sky to sand and sometimes thinning to a slicing razor sharpness, and back again. I fell to my knees, arms still raised. The urge to answer the howl coursed through me as if it were my blood, but I knelt in deliberate silence ten seconds, thirty, longer.

Then I felt silly. I dropped my arms and looked around to make sure no one else in camp had been woken up. Stepping gingerly, first waiting for each swipe of the brush to become cactus, then once I was on the sand imagining every hard speck under my foot to be something sharp and poisonous, I made my way back to the tent. I crawled through the flap I'd left unzipped.

The tent smelled of our family's sweat, a sweet familiar scent with something in it like toast, espresso, bike grease, daisies, and Play-Doh. If I closed my eyes, I might have been standing at home in our kitchen on any evening, a mess of crayons and dolls on the table from Natalie's play, the scraps of dinner throwing their odors out of our garbage can, Beth standing behind me.

Lying on her left side, right arm splayed out of her tiger sleeping bag, Natalie clutched her special prize from our visit to the tourist shop: a round wooden box about the size of a matchbook, which the tag had informed us was an "Authentic Native American Dream Box" capable of making any written wish stored within it come true.

"I want a real kitty," Natalie had divulged after the purchase. "An alive one that always plays and never grows up."

"I'm not sure that's one wish," I'd said, looking for a loophole. "What do you think, Beth?"

But Beth hadn't answered me. She'd been holding the dream box, turning it over and over in her hands before opening the lid to peer in.

Natalie stirred, kicking her feet against the tiger's grasp, maybe dreaming of eternal kittens, maybe reliving that day's cactus disaster. The nostrils of Beth's nose flared as she sensed a disturbance in her daughter's life.

I wanted those ten points.

I was not my father, but no matter how little I was like him I was too much like him.

It was true that I could will myself to be an adequate and perhaps even a good father without the illogical talisman of those points. It was also true that, however distant the dream of scoring ten points had seemed all season, it was by now as out of my reach as the Kaibab moon that had floated above my head. There would be just ten races left by the time we returned home, and by the time I would prove myself in the early race and earn a promotion back to the real thing, there might be only half that. But something, some emotion or awareness or yearning as inexplicable, awkward, and embarrassing, and yet as real as what I had just experienced out there on the lip of the Grand Canyon, made me incapable of swallowing this defeat.

seventeen

WHEN I ROLLED UP TO THE VAN TO PAY MY ENTRY FEE, the two racers in front of me, in full matching kit from helmets to socks, with bikes worth a couple grand each, were discussing how unappetizing their lunch had been—at summer camp. I guessed they were maybe twelve.

It was early evening of the first Thursday in July, and I was suited up and ready to roll around the parking lot for my warm-up, just as I'd done every Thursday since spring. But I wasn't doing the Crit. I was there half an hour sooner than usual, so I could do the early race.

The kids paid and rolled away. I pushed my left foot against the ground and, still resting my right thigh over the top tube, rolled up to Chip and braked. He was sitting in the open back doorway of a white van. There was a cash box on the van floor to his right and a clipboard on his knee. He was already dressed to race, in a Bike Line team jersey and black shorts over long, lean legs that brought to mind a pair of scissors. He had his hand stuck out awaiting cash, but was looking down at the clipboard as I handed him the four one-dollar bills I'd pulled from the rear pocket of my jersey. He said, "Number?"

When I said, "One-nineteen," he looked up. All the early race numbers started with a two or a three.

Chip was one of the old men of the pack, a fifty-plusser. He'd missed the past few weeks. In another race, he'd gone down and lost some skin, but had gotten away essentially unhurt until another racer rode over his back and broke his scapula. Chip had marks from the guy's chainring, a neat little row of perforations, down one side of his body. He said, "Bill."

I said, "Yeah." I gestured around me at the kids warming up, the novice women, the rank beginners, and the Cat 5s— the riders who either had brand-new licenses or were mired at the absolute bottom level of the sport. I'd score lots of points in this race. My friend Ken, one of those lucky people who was blessed with genetic ability, had just begun racing again after not touching a pedal since college—and thus was currently just about as fast as me. He was racking up so many points in the early race that soon he'd have the fifty that were required to be promoted. I'd score ten points in a single early race. But they would not be the ones I needed. They were not the kind of points that could end a curse. "I'm doing the early race," I said to Chip.

"What are you talking about? Are you injured?"

"No. I got, you know. I got dropped."

"You got dropped."

"A couple weeks ago."

Chip flipped some pages and looked at some boxy charts,

red ink, smears of blue. He shook his head. "Well, you can't do the early race. I'm not letting you in it."

I was out completely. My mouth went too dry to swallow.

"Come on, Bill," he said. "You belong up with the fast guys." He flipped a page and there were the names for the late race, in numerical order. He ran his finger down the list until he got to mine, and he said, "One-nineteen. Late Race. Strickland. Get out of here."

I rode away, peeled to the right, and crossed the street to the parking lot of the velodrome. I looped through it counterclockwise, wondering what had just happened, what Chip had seen in me during the races that I hadn't. I coasted around the parking lot. My freehub clicked like a drumroll. I was back in the late race, the real thing, the Thursday Night Crit, the dream quest. I had all the time in the world again—half a season to score ten points.

The gate of the chain-link fence that surrounded the velodrome was open. There was a rider's locker room in there, much nicer than the port-a-pots across the street I'd been using all season. I snapped my bike up onto the sidewalk, dismounted, then clickity-walked into the men's room.

There were walls of lockers in there, puddles on the floor, three urinals, some stalls, two sinks, and mirrors. It smelled gamey. A toilet flushed, a stall door opened, and the Animal came out, carrying his jersey in one hand while pulling the straps of his bib shorts up over his shoulders with the other.

I lifted my chin and nodded. "Hey."

The door behind us creaked, let daylight in. Someone clicked in and walked past me to the urinals, and I became conscious that I might accurately be described as loitering in a men's locker room. The Animal pulled his jersey on, snorted some snot through his nose and into his throat, then spat into the sink. The other guy grunted.

I was still nodding my head. I put my foot on the wooden bench that sat between rows of lockers and leaned over to inspect it. "I got a little shoe thing going on here," I said, and began fiddling with the Velcro straps. While my face pointed floorward, diligently analyzing the straps of my footwear, I heard the Animal clack past me. The door creaked open and shut. The urinal flushed. The other rider clacked out. The door protested once more, and the pulsing of my heart broke against my eardrums.

Despite what Chip had said, I didn't belong. I had never belonged. My manic sprints and erratic strategies and spectacular flame-outs had been the antics of a poser. I could shoot myself through the front of the pack, but I could not ride there. The whole season had been something my accursed forebears would have cheered—a heroic caper against such overwhelming odds that my excuse for failure had been built in before I'd begun. I hadn't been chasing ten points. I'd been, once more, teaching myself to be a Strickland.

Out on my bike again, coasting counterclockwise while my freehub ticked furiously away, granted a second chance at destroying a curse I'd inadvertently nurtured, I wondered what would happen if I tried to live up to what Chip had said. What if my goal was simply to belong—to become just one more bike racer in a whole pack of them? I knew everything I needed to know about how to be a spectacular disaster. I knew nothing at all about how to belong to anything.

I had roughly ten Crits left, depending on rain. The first half of the season had shown me clearly that the point I'd scored last year had been a fluke and that I might stumble into another point amid one of my desperate strafes, but that I'd never get close to ten unless I found a new strategy. The racers who belonged—not the best ones who could score points at will, but the riders who never got dropped, who made it into breakaways, who could rub elbows and converse and even joke with the best—I'd been trying to beat them. I needed to become one of them. I didn't know exactly what that meant, or even if I'd recognize the moment when it came. I didn't know if it would take two races or ten. But until it happened, I knew there was no real use in thinking about ten points. It meant diminishing my quest into a goal. It didn't sound as thrilling or romantic. But it sounded possible.

And that's how I began what I came to think of as my apprenticeship of belonging. For six Crits, from July to the end of August, I stayed within the pack even when I felt I might be able to leave it behind. By not blowing myself apart with all-out efforts, I found that I was able to conserve enough energy to sit in for the entire race. I relentlessly followed the Animal's wheel, trying to comprehend his curious motivations as he scratched apart the pack to stage one of his sprints, or one of his withering charges designed to form an elite breakaway that could stay out front for an entire race. When he launched a move, I'd follow him for a few pedal strokes, then sit up and drift back to the pack, making sure I never blew up, always reserving enough energy to let me follow another wheel and continue my tutelage on the next lap. I restricted myself to a

short list of riders besides the Animal who were worth following: Torch, the elder Simes, Sarah Uhl, Bobby Lea, Bill Elliston. I was an odd character for those two months, always at
the front and always seeming to be full of energy I never used,
occasionally allowing myself to ride along the fringes of a
points sprint, but even then being deliberate about conserving
my power. I didn't want to score points. I wanted to see how
points were scored—and be able to remember it.

I sat in at the front and watched the racers up there make
the pack shudder with its own effort, as if they were putting
the race itself—the entity of the race—under extreme stress, like
one of those old *Star Trek* episodes where, to save itself, the
Enterprise has to go so fast it buckles at its seams. I sat in, hidden from the summer wind that was brutal and relentless for
those two months, and watched how the air blew across the
race course and scattered the riders at the edges of the pack
like dandelion seeds. From following the Animal, I learned to
find a draft where there seemed to be none, to slot my wheel
beside another, to adjust my bike back and forth and sideways
a half inch at a time until I found the tiniest oasis of still air. I
followed the Animal as he returned from breaks and from
scoring points, hacking and coughing and spitting up the re-
fuse of his effort as he drifted back through the pack to recover, and by beginning to understand his riding style, I began
to understand a little of him. Everyone swore, from the way
the Animal rode, that he must be raging against something—
his age or some insecurity or long-ago slight he'd been unable
to let go, or those blessed with more talent but less viciousness
or whatever. But it was just the opposite. Somewhere in his
long career, he'd ridden beyond his own ambition. Although I

doubted he could explain it, the Animal desired purity for the sport. He could not allow the race to not let the fastest, most skilled, most fortunate rider of the day win. When beat, he sounded both pissed off and proud as he praised the victors.

I was able to talk to the Animal without awkwardness after that, sharing the mix of meaningless patter and deep discussion of strategy that lubricates the pack. Sometimes he would drift all the way back to the tail itself to recover, and the riders who resided there greeted us with a wide-eyed, pasty-mouthed awe—him because he was the Animal and me because I was with him, because he was talking to me, telling me what had happened. The Animal had no need to push or shove when he was back there. The riders of the tail opened a zone of respect all around the Animal, as if he were surrounded by a fleet of invisible bodyguards. They would not speak to him, but they would say things to me, like, "windy today," or "you guys are killing us," the kind of things I'd once said, words meant to be sacrificial offerings of humility.

I made riding friends back there and up front, too. The leaders of the pack began recognizing me, now that I lived consistently among them rather than streaking through once or twice a race. There was Ray, who'd weighed 205 while lifting weights and playing lacrosse at Slippery Rock U, but had distilled himself to 180 in only his second season of riding and was already faster than me. There was a guy who always wore a purple jersey, whose calves looked like Popeye's forearms, and who rode with a stillness that was so complete it was unnerving but, when spoken to, would enthusiastically discuss the wind as if we were stockbrokers charting the market. There was Ben Barczewski, a second-generation talent in a star-spangled national-team jersey, a kid who one day was talking about video games as he pulled me along breathless at 35 mph. Torch, whose awareness of the pack was deeper than anyone except maybe Simes the Elder, quickly realized I had devoted myself to the vivisection of drafts. Amused by my study, he would ask me how the drafting was going and sometimes bark directives at me: Left. Right. Up. A few times he put a hand on my back to maneuver me into a draft no logic could detect.

I was not alone in my diligent pursuit of dreams that summer. Natalie's wish, for the kitten that always played and never grew up, had been written down the day we returned home and tucked tightly in the dream box, which sat on the stained blue top of her dresser. She checked the box every morning to see if it had been opened or if there was a kitten somehow contained within it. Many mornings she'd sweep the entire house for the magic kitten before having breakfast. And one day Beth called me at work from her office and said, "Listen to this," then read from her computer screen: "The Singapura is the world's smallest breed of domestic cat. Full-grown, they are often no more than four pounds. Because they have become habituated to living in drain pipes in their native country, they love to crawl under covers and sleep with their owners. They remain playful and affectionate throughout their adult lives, preferring a lap to their own bed."

"You have been looking for the dream cat," I said.

"Yeah." There was a embarrassed enthusiasm in Beth's voice, as if I'd caught her dancing in her underwear or singing in front of a mirror. "I guess so."

"Wow," I said.

"I feel like we promised her the cat when we let her buy the box," Beth said, recovering some of her composure.

"I'm not sure that was included in the purchase price."

"Probably not. Keep listening: They are extremely rare outside of Singapore."

"Oh."

"Kittens often fetch upward of fifteen hundred dollars."

"Next dream," I said.

There was the Crit where the pack became an ocean around me, not only the thing I moved through but also my atmosphere and my source of sense. The holding of a wheel, the slipping of elbows, the thrust of an acceleration all felt necessary, as if because the pack did it I could not do otherwise. Our movements felt not exactly preordained, but something more like inevitable, and I was anticipating each piece of choreography by absorbing signs I could not consciously identify— maybe a tilt of Torch's head or the way the Animal replaced his water bottle after taking a drink. I was never sure what signals I was interpreting. I only knew that I had begun to foretell the key movements of the race. I had become the tongue of the snake but, even then, granted that power, I kept to my plan and retreated before the mouth swallowed the mice that scurried ahead of us. That was not my function, nor my right.

There was the Crit where Bill Elliston and Bird jumped as I sat on their wheels, and around the curves and up the hill and over it we built a forty-foot gap. When it was my turn to ride at the front, I did a ten-stroke pull, then waggled my right elbow to tell Elliston, who was drafting me, that I was coming off. As he passed, I said, "I'm going back." There were one and a half laps to go for points, and as I hovered for a few seconds in the space between them and the pack, I had a smash of regret that I hadn't tried to stay. But then Elliston sat up and looked back, and Bird sat up, and the pack ran up around me and the race came back together. I never knew if my decision to fade into the pack had factored into Elliston's choice. I only knew that while he and I had come to the same conclusion, I'd done so two seconds earlier. It was an odd victory for me, an elusive triumph to know that I was somehow a better rider because I had simply and without fanfare abandoned a breakaway, but it was irrefutable. I'd behaved exactly like a racer. No one watching from the sidelines could have appreciated or understood that. Many of those suffering at the back of the pack never would either. And there was no way to explain such a thing to a five-year-old girl. But what I'd done meant more to me, and to my journey toward ten points, than if the break had stayed away and I'd scored a haphazard point.

Natalie rode home with me in the truck nearly every week. She told me she liked it now that I was racing up front because I was easier to spot. She made up songs about the races. She asked, every week with increasing intensity in her voice, because even she could sense the end of the season, why I hadn't scored a point. I kept telling her I wasn't trying to yet.

Sometimes she said, "Okay," and sometimes she'd ask, "When will you try?" Once, she asked, "So then why are you racing now?"

I said, "I'm becoming a racer."

She nodded and said, "So when you are being a racer you will score ten points."

"That's the plan."

She said, "I have a plan to get my kitty."

"What's that?"

"I wrote my dream down and put it in my dream box."

"That's a good plan. It's simpler than mine."

"I know."

"You know, your stuffed kitties never grow up," I said. In her search for a Singapura, Beth had applied the religious fervor she reserved for chores, but was having no luck. "Maybe sometimes a dream can be finding out you already have what you want."

"Daddy." She sighed. She looked out the window. "The dream kitten I wished for is alive."

"I know. I was just thinking."

"Listen: If it never grows up, will it always live?"

"I don't think so, honey. You didn't ask for it to live forever. Wishes can be pretty literal."

"It will die?"

"Someday."

"Before or after I die?"

"Before."

"Oh."

I drove. She looked out the window, then turned to me and said, "Daddy."

"Yes?"

"Before or after you die?"

"Before."

"And you will die before I die."

"Yes."

"Okay." I could see her working out the timeline, mathematics flicking around behind her eyes. She said, "Daddies die before their kids die. Like Mommy's daddy."

"Yes, beautiful girl. He died just a few months before you were born." She knew this, but liked hearing it confirmed for some reason.

"Your daddy died."

"Yes."

"When did your daddy die?"

"A long time ago."

"But when?"

"When I was still in school."

"Not pre-school."

"No. College."

"Were you very sad? I would be so so so sad you don't even know."

I was still wearing my racing undershirt and my bibs, though I'd shucked jeans over them. My racing socks were still wet on my feet. I didn't answer Natalie. Instead I said, "I smell bad, huh?"

"How sad were you?"

I watched the car in front of us flick its brake lights on, off, on for a long glide to a stop. I said, "I was washing dishes at a restaurant—it was my job—and my mom called—Grandma Mama—and I kept washing dishes."

"Does doing dishes make you sad because you bemember?"

"Sometimes."

"But lucky we have a dishwasher."

I laughed. The car in front of us began moving.

"Do you miss your daddy?"

"Very much," I said, the answer I was supposed to give, but which was not true—especially since Beth and Natalie and I had created our little family. I was, in fact, relieved that his death meant he'd never be able to get anywhere near us. But now I wondered if I missed anything about him enough that I'd wish him alive if I could. I came up with only one thing: Now that I was a father, and knew what it was to love a child, what would I say to him about what he'd done to me?

If only for that chance, although I had no idea what I would tell him, I did, in a way, miss him.

I said it: "Yeah, Boo. I miss him."

"I'm missing him, too," Natalie said. "That's not usual, right, Daddy? I didn't know him and I'm missing him."

"Oh, I think it's usual," I said, only because I loved her use of the word. Then I said what I really wanted to. "I'm glad you're missing him. I hope you keep missing him."

There was the Crit where Jack Simes rolled up beside me at the start and said, "How you feeling?" and I was too surprised to answer him right away. He said, "I just fixed my handlebar tape," and I said, "Good. I mean I feel good. I mean it's also good that you fixed your tape. I didn't mean that was not good." And for once I was nearly happy when the whistle startled me and I fumbled my foot as I tried to click into the pedal, ending up far behind Simes before I'd taken a single stroke.

That night in the truck, after Natalie asked if I'd gotten a point and I said no, and she said she loved me anyway—one of her recurring jokes—I said, "I love you, too."

She said, "I love you three."

"Did you make that up?" I asked.

"No. I heard it."

"At school?"

"Daddy." She shrugged. "I don't know."

"Well," I said, "I love you four."

"I love you fivesixseveneightninetenleventwelve," she said, getting up to twenty-six.

I said, "I love you twenty-seven."

She frowned and chewed her lip, and kicked the dashboard, searching for the twenty-eight in her head, nearly retrieving it, losing it, getting angry, then sad. After a few seconds she stopped kicking and said, "I love you the very last number."

I shot a look over at her as I drove.

"Did you hear that somewhere?" I asked.

"No."

"Don't kick the dashboard. I love you the very last number plus one. Numbers can go on forever. It's called infinity."

"Not forever."

"Yes, forever."

She began kicking the dashboard. "Wrong."

"Sorry, right." I put my hand on her kicking calves. "Stop."

"You are wrong."

"Afraid not."

"You are afraid yes," she said, and began kicking the dashboard again.

"Goddammit, Natalie, stop kicking the dash," I said. "Look, don't make this a big deal."

"There's a last number," she said. "How could there not be a last number? How can you not know it? You don't know how bad you make me feel." She gave the dash a final kick.

162

I drove for a while, then, to make up, I said, "Boo."

"What."

"I love you ten points."

"Wrong," she said.

"Come on, Boo," I said.

"You said you are not trying to score ten points. Right now you love me zero points."

There was the Crit when I let Ray's wheel pull me into a break with Elliston, and when we got a gap and were alone on the hill the three of us looked at each other. I said, "What do you think, Ray?"

Elliston and Ray eyed me. Although Ray was about two inches taller than me, his bulk made him look squat and square. Next to the chiseled, graceful lines of Elliston, he looked like a block of rock a sculptor had gotten bored with. They were made from the same material, but inspired completely different feelings. Ray said, "I just got back from a two-week vacation." That was a no, and we waited for the pack to come to us.

There was another rainy Crit in there, with big, black clouds impaling themselves on the trees, the air damp and the wind even more so, the sky like a jiggling water balloon falling toward us.

"We're going to try to get this in," Chip said, giving his rain speech. "If you come around and the judges are gone, the race is over." There was laughter all around—knowing up in the front, resigned in the middle, nervous in back. Maybe 25 minutes in, big plops came down, and when Elliston accelerated I was there, my tires slipping across paint stripes slick as ice, the spray from his wheel coating my face and shooting up into my nose. Beth was standing by the finish the first time we went around, getting soaked, her shirt darkening and plastering itself over the top of her shoulders, around her breasts, flat against her stomach. The whole time I followed Elliston's attack, I was picturing the hollow at the base of Beth's throat and the long, narrow valleys formed by her collarbones, a hallucinatory lull that ended only when Elliston and I came around the corner for the sprint, so clear of the group I couldn't even see them behind us, and we both noticed that the judges were nowhere to be seen, either. Elliston sat up. I coasted beside him and looked over at him and he gave a shrug and a smile. I said, "Perfect. I don't want points."

That night Beth said, "Did you tell Natalie her new kitten was going to die before it grows up?"

"No. I mean, I don't think so. I said it would die. But—"

"She's convinced her kitten is going to die before it grows up."

"I don't think I said that." But I couldn't be sure. I knew we'd had that talk after a race, a time when Natalie was often sharper than me.

"You have to be careful what you say," Beth said. "This is a big deal to her. She believes in this."

We eyed each other in that searching manner of couples who have been together long enough to weigh the worthiness of having a fight—each trying to figure out how serious the other was, how deep our own commitment to our platform of grievances was, and to what ultimately irresolvable issues this fight might eventually lead: I was sloppy. Beth was neurotically neat. I was self-centered. Beth was stingier than me when it came to charities. I'd drilled an ugly, white-trash hole through the kitchen countertop to pass the wine refrigerator's power cord through. Beth thought pewter was a contemporary color.

"Look," I said, "obviously I believe in dreams."

"You believe in some dreams, obviously."

"What's that mean?"

"Nothing."

"Goddammit . . ." In the pause, I had time to realize that I should say something about how I'd felt at the race that day, about what had been constant in my head since then, the image of her standing there beside the course, soaking wet, lurid and romantic. Instead, I said, "At least I fucking dream, Beth."

Her face arranged itself into an expression of both anger and sorrow. She blinked several times, shook her head, and said, "Thanks." We eyed each other, and stalked off to different parts of the house.

As we lay in bed that night, I kissed Beth's mouth, her nose, her forehead then each eye, and said, "I'm sorry. I'm just trying to get through this." She nodded, tipping her head up and down on the pillow, but didn't say anything. When we sleep, Beth flows her body against me, except when she's angry. That night her elbows and knees were all sharp angles and points. It was like trying to sleep next to a pile of Pick-Up Sticks. I opened a space between us, but kept one hand on her shoulder, in her hair. A long time later, in the dark, so soft I might have imagined it, Beth whispered, "I dream."

And I understood what I already should have—that whatever form Beth's promise to Natalie ended up taking when it came out of that tiny round box, it would be as much for my wife as for my daughter. And from there I understood, in an instant, what I'd never been able to figure out and Beth had never verbalized: Why she hadn't left me, or let me leave, after the affair. When Beth had been in her teens, and her parents were just beginning the divorce that would cost the family its farm and split them between states and homes, her father had come into her room late one night, wearing a jean jacket that smelled of the earth, crunching a toothpick between his teeth. Her hero had sat on her bed and hugged her tight and said, "Whatever happens, I promise I won't let this family come apart."

Beth kept contacting cat breeders, which we found out were called catteries. The few that had even heard of Singapuras all had the same few stories: All our Singapura kittens are spoken for. We won't have Singapura kittens again this year. There's a two-year wait list. In California, Massachusetts, Oregon, it was all the same. Through a series of four or five private referrals, Beth tracked down one male, but it had a heart condition—perhaps the kitten that would make my unwitting prophecy about never growing up come true. We passed. She found an available female, but for $1,000. We'd paid $5 for Jasper and adopted Milo from a cat shelter.

And there was the final Crit in August, when, at the corner before the hill, the wind hit like a hammer to the head—a sensation I truly knew and could vouch for—so someone attacked there on every lap. After fifteen or so rounds of the wind and the surge and the climb, the pack split at the hill and the Animal and four others got away. You could see them working seamlessly, reeling off short, fast, hard pulls as they shrunk down into their bikes to hide from the wind. They opened a quarter-mile gap.

Back in the group, Ray organized a chase—himself, me, Bird, and a bleachy-blonde foreign chick rotating off the front, the four of us pulling the rest of the pack in turns. When one of us came off the lead position and drifted back, whichever of the stragglers was in the fifth position would ease up to open a gap so we could slot back into line in fourth. Over and over and over we ran through the pattern. Every time I pulled, we got a little closer to the Animal's group—just a few feet, but it was something. Then the gap would expand again.

The efforts at the front were delicious, ravaging burns, as if I'd finally learned to like the way whiskey felt going down my throat. And I'd come off and float backward blank, happy, drunk with the pure joy of pulling the pack. It was like a flume ride at an amusement park—each turn at the front drenched me with adrenaline and that overwhelming, whooshing noise of a moving pack. Once as I came back, Ray looked over at me, his head turned and tilted in the sideways and forward position that lets you see up and out at once. He shouted, "Strickland!"

"What?"

He screamed, "Yeah!"

I said, "Screw this. Let me spring you. Blow myself up. Take you within fifty feet. Then you can bridge solo."

Ray shook his head and shouted, "Strickland!"

I said, "What? What the hell?"

"I'm telling you who the hammer is tonight."

And it blew through me, right then, as instantly and decisively as I'd understood how little I understood about Beth that night in bed. At 37 mph, my elbow and handlebar tapping against a guy I knew little else about except that he was called Ray and he was fast, and both of us trusting our health and our $5,000 bikes to a guy in front of us with an avian nickname, I understood bicycle racing.

You were nothing without the pack. Alone, lacking context, you were neither strong nor weak, not stupid or savvy, not inexperienced or innocent or wobbly or feral or graceful or heavy like unfinished statuary. Two months ago, I was slow because the pack was faster. Tonight I was fast because my pack was slower. The pack created its own context and within the pack that was the only context that mattered. I had eaten shit. Paul Pearson, the legendary Animal, was pushing fifty and just a few weeks ago had been telling me how he was picking up cash by temping as a stonemason's assistant. Gibby the Bear, the beloved villain of an entire nation, who'd sown fear and awe into the best professional keirin racers in the world, found himself terrifying Cat 5s in a training race for a shot at a free pizza once a month. The pack didn't care. We were nothing to the pack except the things we did that day.

I was thirty-nine years old. I had been a father for five years and a husband for twelve, and for the first time in my life, I belonged to something.

I was ready to score points.

eighteen

NATALIE'S DREAM WAS CALLED FRIED RICE.

The kitten's real name was Shiverdeen's Jubilee Girl. "Shiverdeen's Jubilee" was her pedigreed mother, and "girl" was a generic tag used by breeders. But, her original owners told us, for all four months of her life, the three-pound kitten had been known by her nickname, an homage to the color of her short fur.

"Look at this," Beth said, walking up behind me and putting a color picture from a laser printer in front of me as I sat at the kitchen table one evening near the end of July. Nat was in the bathtub. "Adorable, huh?"

The kitten's huge eyes dominated its head, as if it had been drawn by a Disney artist or a child. There was something in its stance, in the curve of its coiled hind legs and tilt of its ears, that conveyed mischief and a kind of consternation to be among people who didn't share its sense of humor.

As I absorbed both the image of the Singapura and the significance of the fact that Beth was walking around with pictures of it, I asked, "Have we already bought this cat?"

"Not technically," Beth said.

"Which means that—"

"It means that we can make a dream come true for Natalie."

"Yes."

"It means, Mr. Ten Points, that we can instill in her the idea that it's okay to wish for much from life and ask much—"

"I know," I said, holding a hand up in surrender to my own ridiculously high-minded statements. "By the way, I really believe all that garbage."

"Me too." Beth put her arm around my shoulders and brought her head next to mine.

Hearing her speak of dreams, I'd been struck by how I must have sounded all these months. Boisterous, pretentious, unsophisticated. Unmoored. Speaking that way to a child was one thing. But being in the presence of an adult who talked to another adult about wishes, innocence, belief—it made me feel full of possibility and wonder, and a little fear, as if the world I looked out at from inside my body were still unfathomable and full of mysterious rules, the way it must feel when we are newborn. Beth and I and everyone we knew worked long hours, then talked too much about our jobs when we got together at parties. We watched the news on TV and surfed the Web to stay abreast of the planet's ongoing dramas, from celebrity heartbreak to war, as if the Earth were a troubled old friend we all had in common. Great books and movies could still shift our hearts within our bodies, but in a few hours the tide of our day would settle everything back into its place and the art that once might have changed our lives was just one more thing to talk about when we ran out of news. We all monitored mortgage rates and invested time in trying to puzzle out the best insurance plans, deals on new gutters, or which hours the grocery store would be least crowded. It seemed as if Beth and I sometimes went, like every couple I knew, long weeks without remembering in a conscious way that we were married to someone we loved, or that chicken vindaloo was our favorite Indian dish not because it was our favorite but because if you really paid attention when that taste washed over your tongue, that was as good as anything ever got.

None of us was without taste buds, or desires so powerful and primal they should frighten us as much as they thrilled us. But we got through our lives by insulating our emotions and sensory perceptions, and of course it was the right thing to do. How the hell could you clear your e-mail in the morning if you succumbed to the infinite pleasure to be found within a banana muffin? We would not be able to function as adults if we followed the lush and twisted pathways of our longings, or even spent too long gazing down them. We might trail a finger across our dreams when we got boozy, or when someone we knew got fired or died, or when a song we once loved came on the radio. Then it was back to life.

A family curse that could be broken with a bicycle. A kitten that never grew up—and a wife who believed in such a thing. To speak aloud of such totems risked robbing them of their power, rendering them into something cute, perhaps even touching, but ultimately meaningless, a child's crayon drawing you threw away after a few days of display on the refrigerator.

Sharing our dreams so openly with each other felt as intimate as making love.

Three pounds of Fried Rice was shipped to us at the end of August. We had to sign a contract that promised all sorts of things: We attested that we would not let said Singapura roam outside and that we would have her spayed by a specified date; we agreed that we could not sell or give her away, except to the original owner or with the original owner's consent. If the Singapura was found at any time to be undernourished or mistreated or neglected—I briefly imagined someone from the cattery clandestinely flying to Pennsylvania and peeking through our windows for verification once or twice a year—we would forfeit her back to the buyer. We were signatories to the vow that we would take Fried Rice née Shiverdeen's Jubilee Girl to the vet regularly. There was even a clause where we promised to give the cat "human attention."

On a Sunday night around 8:00, I took our unsuspecting daughter into our room to read books before bedtime. Nat was allowed to sleep with Beth and me once a week, what she'd designated her "big-bed night." As she clambered up onto the bed with a stack of literature, from *Where the Sidewalk Ends* to one of those fat-cat-rat beginner books, I closed our bedroom door. While we read, Beth drove to the airport.

I was reading a poem about a hairy, scary giant when I heard Beth pull into the garage. The door to our mudroom opened and closed. Steps came down the hall. I finished the poem and began examining its picture, pointing out the creature's frightening details to cover the sound of Beth creeping into Natalie's room, releasing the kitten onto her bed and, as planned, removing the paper wish from the dream box, then turning the container on its side with the lid off.

Beth opened the door to our room.

"Mommy!" Nat cried and jumped to her feet. She trampolined on the bed twice then into Beth, who took a step backward, bracing herself and absorbing Nat's momentum. Beth had left the light on in Natalie's room, and across the dark hallway we could see it limning the edges of her door. Natalie, who had inherited her mother's obsessive caretaker gene, noticed it, as Beth had predicted she would.

"Hey," Natalie announced. "My light is on." She clambered down out of Beth's arms and stomped toward her room.

I rose from the bed and Beth and I stood in the frame of our door, watching our daughter walk toward her dream. She grasped the doorknob and swung the door open, then turned left to switch her light out.

Her jaw dropped. I'd never seen that happen in real life, had always assumed that was just an expression. But as Natalie stood there, frozen, her jaw literally fell open, as if it had become unhinged. That was her only movement. She didn't even blink.

She closed her mouth.

Her jaw dropped again.

Then she screamed.

"My kitten's here! She came!"

Natalie disappeared from the frame of the door and a few seconds later reappeared, running to our room with her arms clutched around a kitten that would never grow up and would always remain playful.

My breath caught and life stopped, granting us time to savor the moment and etch it into ourselves. Natalie, arms basketed in front of her with the kitten upright in them and gazing serenely out at us, our daughter's mouth open in a big O that raised her cheekbones up into half-circles under her rounded, popping blue eyes. And then there was an overwhelming flurry of motion and tears and trembling shouts of affirmation masquerading as disbelief, of kitten being shoved into and out of our arms, the moment a big, wild scribbling of crayon that we would never throw away.

Later, after the pandemonium and the hundred recountings of how she'd seen the kitten pouncing across her bedsheets, and after we'd examined the dream box for clues, and after Natalie had fallen asleep with the kitten, as advertised (but not, I remembered, guaranteed by law in the contract), curled up and purring against her under the covers—and for weeks and months and years after that night, Natalie would tell anyone who'd listen that her kitten Bella had leaped out of a dream box.

But that first night, as Natalie and the dream kitten lay sleeping between us, Beth whispered, "What do you think will happen when she finds out?" Even in the faint light coming from the hall I could see doubt in my wife's eyes about the way we'd brought the kitten into our lives. "Will she think dreams are a fraud?"

I wasn't worried at all. I'd already thought long and hard about the day when Natalie was old enough to look at the score sheets from my magical season of bike racing and see that her father's impossible ten points were surpassed in a single race by a number of cyclists.

"She'll stop believing in dream boxes," I said. "She'll start believing in the people who fill them."

nineteen

WHEN THE SECOND POINTS SPRINT OF CRIT 16 CAME, it was as if I threw myself into a fire to save myself from drowning, but I'd been waiting for this chance—not so I could score, but to tack myself onto the big attack that, since the whistle, I'd sensed was going to come at this moment. Ray was there with me in the wedge formed by Speedy and Torch and the Animal, his exhaust bellowing out in a rhythm that matched mine but was half a beat ahead. Bleachy Blonde Foreign Champion Chick kept snicking her front wheel between us like a fillet knife. Behind her: Purple Jersey and a streaking melting mass of color I knew we were going to ride away from.

Up onto the hill, lined out single file, no looking back, no sitting up, no chatter, no nothing but the churning of our pedals, as if we were a machine laying fresh black pavement between us and whoever might care to chase. I'd made the selection.

There was no one on my wheel. Nine riders ahead of me. This was the breakaway I'd been waiting for all season. I blew snot between my arm and thigh, grinned. Hurt. Rode. In front of me, the real racers swapped pulls at the front, sucking the rest of us along. I wasn't doing anything until I heard the bell. And then my goal was going to be simple: Hold the Animal's wheel.

The bell clapped its high, frenetic warning two laps later. While the sound waves were still washing over us, I slashed from dead last up the side of the group with no idea how I was going to auger my way in once I reached the Animal, who was sitting third. By pure luck, he picked the instant that I ran even with his rear wheel to juke out of the paceline, coil down onto his bike, and attack. I hadn't taken his wheel; it had been shoved in my face. He towed me past the pack, nothing in front of us but air and the last half-mile of the points lap. I skittered sideways in his draft, searching for the constantly shifting pocket of calm air, but also making sure I could see his hands deep in the drops of his handlebar. The Animal never unintentionally telegraphed—he never betrayed his intention to jump, the way most of us did, by shifting his butt before he sprinted or by wiggling his arms or looking behind him. I had to detect some kind of sign that would give me a chance to anticipate the attack that was coming.

Anything.

My senses bled out of me. I blinked and had to fight to fully raise my eyelids, as if they were rickety blinds in a cheap motel. The Animal's right pinky finger slid a quarter-inch down the curve of his handlebar, then off it, curling inward.

That insignificant movement couldn't possibly mean

anything—yet it was the only motion the Animal's entire body had made that was not poured directly into his bike. I let two pedal strokes go soft to open a small gap I could accelerate into, then sprang forward out of my saddle and emptied myself into the pedals, the whipping of my legs turning my entire year of sacrifice and my months and months of vainglorious drama and my new sense of belonging into some kind of puree of desperation that sprayed out of me, and when the Animal jumped in the final turn, I was already moving faster than he was.

I ran up into his draft. I was going to hit his wheel. I was going to crash. He jumped again. There was road between us. I'd lost his wheel. I crawled like a terrified infant back to the wheel, and he jumped once more and rode away. The rest of the break streamed past me.

I crossed the line tenth, my neck going limp, my head nearly hitting the handlebar as it dropped. But my feet still spun and the sound of gears banged off my head all around, so I knew I was still with the group. From my bowed position, I tried to focus on whatever I could see, and it was my heart rate monitor. The numbers were blurry, as if Vaseline had been smeared across the lenses of my eyes.

I'd done everything right. I'd been perfect, and I was tenth. I belonged, for sure. I belonged with these riders, the top ten racers tonight at the Thursday Night Crit. But I could not score. That thing they had done, that last acid burst of flame somehow finding a fuel that could burn up their bodies after everything had already turned to cinder, that was not only beyond me but beyond what I could imagine creating, let alone enduring.

My eyes cleared. We were on the hill, and I saw that my heart rate was 186. It must have been around 200 at the sprint. My chest felt as if it were being sawed open from the inside. The number on my monitor dropped to 176. I was recovering. The gap ahead of me, the one between belonging in tenth and belonging in fourth, was at least as great as all the distance I'd closed the entire season. There were eighteen laps left in this race. Just four more Crits in the season. And I still lacked the most elusive, yet largest thing—and I had no idea what it was. By this time in the year I could be sure I wasn't short on miles or discipline or desire or speed training or fast new wheels or a groundbreaking strategy. What I was missing was a miracle. I needed something to pop out of a dream box.

The Animal drifted past, fading backward as he recovered, wheezing, hacking, crucified between his saddle and handlebar. Something huge, so green it was black, came out of his mouth and splatted onto the pavement, then was whisked away as the asphalt spooled beneath us. Without raising his head, the Animal turned his face toward me. It was magnificent in its collapse—the majesty of a cavern instead of a mountain. The poise with which he bore his ruination reminded me of something else that I could remember existed, but not recall.

There was a hole deep within the hole of his face, and the edges of it curled out and around the ragged corners of each breath he took, a strange, almost tender action, as if he were suckling the air itself. His head swiveled back down facing the ground, drooping between his forearms, which were laid across each brake hood. As if to complete the image of supplication, as we pedaled along the darkening asphalt, the Animal's head and chest bobbed in time to each revolution of his feet.

And I understood.

The bicycle racer beside me was not begging for recovery to come, or for mere survival, or even for an end to the agony. He was giving thanks that it had happened. He was using it to become stronger, suffering so he could suffer again, to greater depths. I remembered where I'd seen that peculiar nobility before: That day at the Dream Come True Ride, when Natalie had wrecked and we'd had to ride to the car anyway, and I looked back once and saw the same purity of purpose in her five-year-old face.

The Animal had no need to endure suffering. He embraced it.

My father had been making me eat shit, every other week or so, for nearly three months. Sometimes I was wracked for a day or two by stomach cramps, or spent an hour vomiting, or had trouble sleeping. Once, after I'd gone to the bathroom, the bowl had been covered with a scum of thick, creamy pink pus. I often felt as if live things were squirming through my stomach and guts, while I myself, at eleven, was becoming a dead thing.

One day I stared at a plate of shit in front of me, three or four pieces, of which I knew I had to bite off only maybe half of one to serve whatever purpose I was serving and end the episode. I stared at the shit until I could not see it, then I reached out and grabbed every piece with my hand and brought the entire mess to my mouth and popped it all in at once.

I closed my eyes and chewed hard, and fast, with my mouth open, loud and smacking, and I swallowed about half of the stewy mess, then raised my head and opened my eyes and looked at my father sitting all the way across the table watching me.

I said, "Give me more."

Through our lives together, not just during the worst but during the best, I'd seen many things in my father's eyes, some of which a son should see, such as pride and happiness and wonder and plain anger, and some a son should not, such as fury and that bottomless loss. But that moment was the first time I ever looked into him and saw uncertainty. And seeing it, then recognizing it, I felt a rush of power. I swallowed the rest of the pudding of shit, and the gag that followed, then I looked across the wasteland of our dinner table at my father, setting my jaw into a posture that I meant to say, "Give me all you got."

There were two laps to go and I was foaming. It was the Animal and the Bear and Purple Jersey and Torch and Ray and me up and over the hill. The thing we were doing to ourselves, this anguish, might be infinite but it was only infinite vertically, limitlessly deep and high, like an orgasm without borders until it reached its end on the horizontal strip of time and stopped. Its end would come—that was the secret. And, knowing that, I wanted as much as I could get while I could get it.

The Animal was screaming at Torch—"Bruce, give me the fucking wheel"—and Torch was swinging across the asphalt in front of me, maybe at me, and I had no comprehension of what was happening except that I was foaming and the racers were foaming, too, and screaming "pull it through," and "pull off," and "pull over." I was empty, so I stood up and pedaled as hard as I ever had, staggering my way to the front, where I could swallow some more emptiness, because the more I inhaled the hotter I burned it up, and the more I filled myself, the emptier I got. It was as if I'd become so tired I'd gotten faster, as if the energy that had vacated my body had been an immense weight I'd been laboring to carry.

There was more wind. More yelling. We were through the woods and into the corner, and Torch whined past, his legs banging down hard strokes in some weird kind of stop-motion where I could count them—one, two, three, bam, bam, bam—and he was smiling and I was grimacing back. Ray punched through us and the Animal pushed me left and Gibby the Bear pushed me right and everyone passed me, and I wanted more. My hands were in the drops and I was standing. I was passing people.

I passed Ray. I passed Bill Elliston. I was third. There were two foaming screaming racers in front of me and I could see the line. It wasn't running away from me like it always had before. It rushed toward me—the end of infinity. Someone passed me and I was fourth and I slung my feet in circles and flung my mouth open and sucked in all the pain I could, because soon the line would come and my chance to feel this would be over for another week, and the line came to my wheel, and Speedy passed me.

Fifth.

By the width of a tire, one place out of the points.

I stretched across my bike, a skin across its skeleton. There was nothing to me except what was inside, which was bike, and something that was neither exhaustion nor satisfaction but both at once. We coasted. I rose and fell, rose and fell against my bike, like a heaving stomach against the ribs of a fetched-out dog.

181

After a while, someone glided backward toward me, then beside me, and began keeping time with me. I heard the tick of gears at rest, the soft clank of a relaxed chain, the shooshing of tires free from the distressing extremes of traction.

It was Pearson. The Animal. I swallowed, but I was spitless. I gagged, but there was nothing to bring up, either. Skin on a bike.

Pearson smiled that predatory, unnerving, ghastly smile.

And without planning to, I smiled back at him, spit hanging from my lips and dried on both ends of my mouth.

"That's the way," said the Animal. "That's the way you do it, Billy."

twenty

His eyebrows had arched when I'd asked for more. Now they crept down, straightening and elongating until they flat-lined across the slits his eyes had become. The tip of my father's tongue flicked into a corner of his lips then across the bottom one, redrawing his mouth into a thin, lupine smile.

My teeth chattered against each other, but I kept my jaw jutted, breathing through my nose and staring at my father. He was wearing a white-and-blue hockey shirt, one I still have—the only material thing of my father's I possess. The neck was wide and I could see the start of the scar that jagged across his left shoulder, a disturbingly smooth strip of skin with raised borders. At various times, he'd claim to have gotten it from a plumbing repair gone bad, from a fight, from an accident with hydrochloric acid.

A longer, more ragged scar runs the length of my left shoulder, a souvenir from a bike wreck that broke my collarbone. Sometimes when no one else was home, I would dig the faded hockey shirt from under a pile of clothes in my closet and put it on and stare at the scar in a mirror.

His head bobbed ever so slightly, as if he were nodding his head inside his head. It was as if he'd been waiting for this moment for a long time.

"Oh," he said. "We got more." And he turned and walked out of the dining room and into the hallway.

I considered running, through the kitchen and down the three steps and out the screen door, cutting across the walk and through the yard and into the street, and then down the hill and then somewhere. I couldn't imagine where. I sat in the chair and put my forearms on the table, pushing the plate in front of me with my fingertips until it was beyond my reach, then I arranged my arms into a V, interlaced my fingers, and tilted my head to the right, and waited, as if my father were bringing me a surprise for something good I'd done.

The Animal and Elliston laid on their brakes and sat up, slamming the forty-one racers that had come out for Crit 17 back together like an accordion. In the fourth row, where I was, front wheels and whole bikes sprayed up through us, then were sucked just as quickly backward when the leaders re-accelerated.

With only four Crits left, we'd been given a perfect mid-September evening for racing. The wind that had hammered against the pack all summer seemed to have lost its strength. On the horizon past the little hill where so many of us were going to crack, the sun was held aloft by the branches of trees, a source of deep golden light without its usual infernal heat. The infrastructure of my body felt new and strong, as if it had just finished being constructed, and the reserves of energy stored inside me felt deep but fresh, as if they'd just been mixed and poured into me. Before the race, I'd seen Beth and Natalie ahead of me on the path that led to the course, walking with their hands entwined. I'd pedaled up beside Beth, put my hand on her shoulder for balance, coasted. Natalie had been holding the corner of an opened, crinkly bag of snack food in her free hand, and she'd held it up for my inspection. Her hair riffled with the lightest flow of wind that could make hair riffle. Her fingers were dusted with orange powder. I could smell synthetic cheese flavoring. Beth shook her head, shrugged, frowned a smile, and said, "She kept saying she really needed a snack."

"Daddy," said Natalie, as she held a puffy orange curl out to me, "you need a Cheese Curl."

"I need to warm up," I said. I took my hand from Beth's shoulder. But before I applied pressure to the pedal, I'd reached out and down, taken the snack from Natalie, and popped it into my mouth. It vanished, dissipating into nothing as soon as it was inside my mouth, yet it still somehow mysteriously crunched. "A Cheese Curl," I'd said. "Just what I need before a race."

Up front, Elliston and the Animal and Torch and some others just kept climbing through each mph, a steady crawl up the speedometer that never made you feel as if you had to accelerate to stay with them. Instead, you just suddenly realized you were going much faster than you wanted to. It was like being crushed by a steamroller. You were trapped under a slow, flattening, rolling, top-heavy pressure that squeezed the air not only out of your lungs but, cell by cell, asphyxiated your body. I understood that eventually I would be asked to go not only faster than I wanted to, but faster than I physically could. I had a moment of admiration that, this late in the season, the pack had unveiled yet one more new way to race. Then I felt a flutter of something drift backward, the first strain of a change in the tone of someone's pedal cadence, or maybe the tippity tap of a finger against a shift lever, and I rose slightly out of the saddle and stretched my peripheral vision wide and waited for the attack that would burst the pack.

It came. A gap opened in front of me like the roaring jaw of a beast with asphalt at the back of its throat. I dropped my head and drilled into the wind, scooting forward on my bike, the nose of the saddle the only thing touching my ass, and I was pushing back at the pedals instead of straight down onto them, as if I were trying to jump from my bike onto the Animal's back, and it worked. I closed the gap.

I made the break.

There were ten of us, which I did not know until we were all the way around the track again, until we had done a complete lap and were crossing the line and I could function enough to count. The pack was out of sight behind us, somewhere far back in the woods. Pearson sat up, then Elliston and Ray, and Torch, and Purple Jersey, and the rest. Now we would wait.

We would wait for one of us to panic, to lose faith that the chasing pack could not catch us, to crack mentally and take off at full speed for the line—at which time the rest of us would slot into the draft cast by the sacrificial racer, then sweep past for points at the line. We waited. We waited until I knew I had to go, until I was sure we had delayed so long that there was no way the ravenous pack would not come roiling over us at the last instant and ruin my chance for points. But the Animal did nothing, so I did nothing. We waited. I had to go. I rose out of my saddle.

Purple Jersey jumped.

He was gone a long time, long enough for me to stop trying to decode the bumps and door closings I heard, to stop listening for his return, to become aware of the sounds of the house settling and creaking, and then to stop noticing even that. As the last sliver of the afternoon sun slid just past the edge of the sliding glass door and the room around me faded, my eyes adjusted until I sat in a visible darkness. When he emerged from the dark of the hallway, he was carrying a dark washrag, cupped in one hand.

I could smell the fresh, wet shit. It was not dogshit.

He brought his cupped hand to me and held it before my face, under my nose, then dropped the washrag heavy onto the table. The washrag was green. In the few inches it had fallen, the shit had compressed itself and spread wide, here and there shooting slender arms of mottled brown off the washrag onto the surface of the table and my arms.

My father said, "Here we go," and before I could say no or shake my head or recoil or react at all, he cocked his arm at the elbow and reached behind his back and pulled the pistol around and pointed it at my face and pulled the trigger.

It clicked. The sound was low and hard and heavy at first, as if a boulder had dropped onto the floor. Then there were high, shrill metal-on-metal notes, then the tones combined and reverberated, filling the room.

"Empty," my father said. He clicked something on the pistol and flicked it to the side and the cylinder where the bullets were supposed to go flipped out. There were six holes there, empty, like he'd said.

"That, son, was to make sure you believe I'll pull the fucking trigger."

He pulled a brown bullet with a gold tip from the pocket of his Wranglers and held it aloft between us, pointed up, like a missile. His hand shoved the bullet into the top hole and then spun the chamber around. The bullet whirled faster than my eyes could follow. While the cylinder was still whizzing around, clicking like a freewheel—like the sound my bike makes every time I ride it—my father flipped the gun sideways again and the chamber clacked back into the pistol.

"This is a game," my father said, "I played with my dad." He gave out a two-syllable sigh with a choked chuckle buried deep in it. "There are six chambers in here and one bullet. That means there are five empty chambers and one that will fire. Do you understand that?"

I nodded.

"So chances are five out of six I won't blow the back of your head off. Did they teach mathematical odds and ratios in sixth grade?"

I nodded.

"Those are good odds, right? Five out of six."

I nodded.

"Except we don't know where the bullet was when I locked the cylinder in. It might fire the first time I pull the trigger, or the sixth. Or at any time in between, right?"

I nodded.

He said, "Eat." He straightened his arm and pointed the handgun at my face and kind of looked away while still keeping one eye on me. I looked at the pistol, trying to see where the bullet was. I could only see parts of four holes, the ones at the sides.

I shook my head.

Once before, maybe the second or third time he had put dogshit in front of me, I'd refused and he'd put his hand on the back of my head, cupping me in his palm with gentle deliberation, then slammed my face into the plate and held me down there, grinding me against the shit. It had gotten in my nose, stuck in my eyelashes, my eyebrows. I'd eaten almost none of it.

"I'll fucking pull this trigger," he shouted, and his finger twitched against its dark curved surface. I looked hard at the round part of the pistol where there was one bullet somewhere, and I shook my head.

The click was louder than the last one, louder than anything I'd heard in my life, louder than when he'd shot Prince with the sun at my ear, louder than the sound of the hammer hitting me, and louder than the things inside my nose breaking. Louder than anything could be.

I'd pissed my pants. One track of my mind rationally wondered how he would explain the wet, fouled chair to my mother. My hands were still interlaced in front of me, between me and the fetid mound of my father's feces, and I became aware that my arms were vibrating. I began to sob, to snort, and then to whimper, and then, every time I took in a breath, I made a sound, a fractured, high, hollow cry. Spit was blowing out onto my chin, onto my chest, and onto the table between my arms.

"Goddammit," my father said. "Just fucking eat up, Billy."
He was taking steps back and forth, still pointing the gun at me
at arm's length. I was crumpling into myself, but my jaw was
still setting between my breaths and spitty sobs. The waistband
of his jeans bobbed just above my eye level as he stepped forward and back, the hockey shirt tucked in on the left, hanging
loose on the side where his arm had ripped the gun from the
back of his jeans. Then his clothes became still and the gun
came into my face, filled my vision, and dropped away.

Something hard and cold scraped up over my chin and
smashed my bottom lip flat against my teeth. The scraggly
edges of my teeth cut the inside of my mouth, and I pressed
my lips together with as much force as I'd ever done anything
in my life. When the stubby gun barrel couldn't push its way
into my mouth, my father reared it back an inch or so and
popped me in the face with it. I opened my mouth and yelped
and my father shoved the barrel of the pistol in.

I jumped. Shit eater. Adulterer. White trash. It all stripped
away. I was nothing except this jump. The world was nothing
except the ten-foot gap between my front wheel and the wheel
of some guy I knew only by the color of the jersey he wore
each week. My wheels began making a low whooming sound
like a commuter jet's propeller winding up. I'd never made my
bike emit that sound before, but I'd heard it from some of the
others. The hiss of pure power.

I got the wheel. A guy in a KU jersey was on my wheel. Behind him was Blue Jersey, and behind him someone else, some
shadow skipping from side to side. The five of us were all the
way around the track again and past the line and into the

curves, which meant we were on the points lap—though I hadn't heard the bell—and at the hill, halfway around the track, I looked back and we had fifty feet on the Animal's pack.

But his chase group was not just closing on us. They were inhaling the space between us, packing it into themselves as they ate it, growing bigger and stronger and faster until I could see the faces of the Animal and Bill Elliston, and there in the woods, they had caught us.

The gun tasted like the tang of the hammer. And like cinnamon or some sweet spice, like the baking soda my mother sometimes made us brush our teeth with, and like dirt. It tasted blue. It tasted cold. I flattened my tongue against the hole in the end of the barrel, then narrowed the tip into a point and stuck it in. The barrel was very short, a couple of inches at the most, and there was another tiny round piece under it, and both parts clicked off my top and bottom teeth. My head pushed back hard against the chair.

My father had both hands on the gun now, fingers around the handle, a couple over the outside of the trigger guard, and a finger on the trigger. He was shaking. The gun trembled in my mouth and clacked against my teeth. The raised sight guide on the tip kept scraping open the top of my mouth, and little strings of my mouth were hanging down and coming off, and I kept swallowing them.

I had shit liquid in my pants. I was somewhere far beyond tears, beyond snot and whimpers. My father's mouth moved. He was speaking. The gun shook more. My hands went to his arms and glided along them, up to his hands, and I covered them as if we were praying together, my fingers and palms laid upright along his, and from either side my thumbs closed together in symmetry against the finger he had on the trigger.

He, or me, or both of us, pushed against the trigger.

It arced away from me. There was notchy, mechanical movement I could feel through my father's hands. The chamber revolved, and there was a snap that I could not hear but that vibrated through the gun, and the trigger returned to where it had begun. We began pushing against the trigger again.

My father ripped his hands and the gun from my hands and the gun out of my mouth. The barrel was wet and shiny, and my father stumbled backward one step, two, caught his balance and swayed, as if he were about to disintegrate into the helpless creature with bottomless loss for eyes.

I stood and the chair fell backward. I flung out my arm straight at him and screamed, "You knew where the bullet was. You can't kill me. You can't kill me. You can't. You can't. You can't." I repeated myself until I could not remember saying "you can't" the first time or the last. The words wound out of me and around and around the room, an incantation that was as much a revelation as an accusation.

When the Animal blurred through us, I threw my bike from side to side, my hands in the drops and the propeller noise of speed chopping up the air around me. All that was left of me now was the pure act of pedaling. Racing neither hurt nor felt good. I was free. My feet spun circles too fast for the eye to follow. Bird on my left and Elliston on my right leaped past me and leaned in to take the Animal's wheel. I flailed over my bike and stuck my wheel between theirs. My handlebar bumped their saddles. The finish line rushed to me as if it were the ground and I'd jumped off a building. I was fourth and that was going to be good enough for a point, and I didn't dare look sideways to see if anyone was coming to pass me, because even that wasted motion, a flick of the eyes, could cost me my point. The finish line shot into my face and there was a hole, and I passed Bill Elliston, and I was third. I had scored two points.

My father and I stared at each other for a long time, my chest heaving, his shaking, and then I blinked back some tears and locked down my jaw. Holding the gun trembling at his side, he walked out of the room.

twenty-one

"Is it really possible," I asked Beth, "that I can feel like my life has changed because of the order that three other guys and me rode bicycles across a line of spray paint?"

We were sitting on our couch late into the night of the Crit, each with one leg bent yoga-style and the other hanging down to the floor, each staring into the face opposite ours as if we were in college and just getting to know each other. Beth said, "Is it possible for a cat to leap out of a $7.49 souvenir?"

We'd celebrated my two points at dinner—rotini with garlic and sautéed chicken for Beth and me, pasta with a little butter and parmesan cheese from the green shaker bottle (which she liked better than fresh shredded) for Nat, and for all of us Cheese Curls from the cellophane bag that sat in the middle of our kitchen table.

Natalie had kept rattling her hand inside the bag and, every time she pulled out one of the orange puffs, saying, "I told you," or "see." As she put them onto my plate, she kept erupting into a jut-jawed, pursed-lip smile that since the crib had been her sly yet unmistakable expression of pride.

Beth had said, "Better save some. Daddy needs eight more points in three races."

We'd all lingered at the table long past Natalie's bedtime, talking and laughing, teasing each other over our newfound faith in the transformative power of Cheese Curls, and reliving how Natalie had run as fast as she could beside me on one of the remaining laps, her skinny legs whistling past each other in short strides as she shouted, "You got points," before dropping away. After Beth had finally announced, "Teeth, potty, and pajamas," and she and I were alone, I'd said, "I want to tell you something."

"Daddy." Natalie was standing beside us. "Spell 'could.'"

I spelled it and she ran down the hall repeating it to herself.

Beth and I raised our eyebrows at each other. I reached out across the kitchen table and took Beth's hand in mine. I said, "Here's the thing."

"Daddy." Natalie was standing there, holding a scrap of paper and a purple marker out to me. She said, "Write 'could' so I can copy it."

"Okay," I said. "Then—Nat, lights out or no TV tomorrow."

While Natalie had stomped off to her room, having grudgingly decided the morning's cartoon viewership held more value than finishing whatever project she'd embarked on, I'd stared down at my plate: Two Curls, one for each point I possessed.

Charlie Mexico was a friend of my father's, or he worked with him, or was some indefinable distant relation, or a criminal who knew he could find refuge with us—he was just Charlie Mexico, someone who was always around when I was four, five, six. At Wrigley Field one day—not the same time when he allegedly stole the Reds cap off a player—a foul ball had been hit into the stands near our seats. There'd been the usual scrum, and Charlie Mexico had come up out of the pile with the ball. There were some bloody faces, some swollen eyes, spilled beers, wet shirts. There might have been a fight outside the park, as well. I just remember commotion, blurry images of men lunging and retreating, yelling amid the smell of peanuts and beer, then speeding back home to Gary, Indiana, in a convertible. And I remember Charlie, with a huge, tendon-strapped forearm, turning in the driver's seat and holding the ball out to me in the back.

"Can I keep it?" I asked.

"No," he said. No other explanation. But he rolled the ball into my cupped hands. One of his fingers—I think his pinky—stood crooked and apart from the rest. I'd never seen a broken bone before, but I knew that's what it was.

"Wow," I said, about the finger, the baseball forgotten for a moment.

"Fucking maniac," affirmed my father, twisting around in the passenger seat and seeing where I was focused. Charlie Mexico was wheeling through the streets as if we were in a movie, being pursued. We went into a tunnel, or under a bridge. He literally stomped his foot on the gas pedal and the little car seemed to jump up off the road and leap forward, tires squeaking like a plane's landing gear. Charlie Mexico's broken hand pointed at the speedometer on the dash, the needle lined over the number 100, and he said, "See that? See that?"

"Your finger's broken," I said.

Charlie waved the thought off with the injured hand. "It's a fucking finger," he said. "That there is a major-league baseball."

"Yeah." I remembered the treasure in my hands and looked down to appreciate it. There were scuffs on it, and smudges from the bats. A signature. Some of the red threads were frayed. I rubbed it. I smelled it. Charlie Mexico's hand was draped back over the seat, palm up and waiting. The headwind was piling over the windshield of the tiny car, pummeling me, driving me back into the seat whenever I relaxed, and I was afraid the ball would blow away from me when I gave it back to him, so I cradled it in both hands and set it deliberately into his palm.

Charlie Mexico closed his hand and lifted his arm and heaved the ball over his head and out of the car. It caromed wildly off the side of the tunnel, bounced down onto the road, then to the ceiling and back down, then it disappeared behind us. It made knocking sounds, like wood on wood, as it struck the road and walls. Charlie Mexico screamed, "Yeehah, yow, yow, yow!" My father chortled and took a drink from a can of Stroh's as we shot back into full daylight.

Charlie Mexico turned around and faced me again, a wide warrior face, a drunk face ripe with beer and sweat. He said, "Once I decided I wanted that fucking ball, I'd have broken all my fingers to get it."

My father said, "Amen," and toasted Charlie Mexico. Then, with the hand that held the beer, he poked me in the chest with his index finger, and it flattened me back against the seat. Charlie Mexico was watching us. He wasn't watching, at all, where he was going. And, as if he lived in a world that ran thoroughly against my understanding, he compensated for his inattention by pushing against the gas pedal until the little car whined as the speedometer's orange needle fluttered over 100 again.

"It's still just a fucking baseball, Billy boy," said my father. "You can decide stupid shit is worth dying for. But that doesn't make it anything else but stupid shit, right?"

Without waiting for an answer, my father drained his can, crumpled it, and threw it out. Charlie Mexico pivoted away from me and faced the road, the car sped up, and we streamed home full of beer and mysterious, multilayered truths.

As a kid, and into my teens, I'd spent hours trying to decipher what Charlie Mexico and my father had been telling me. Was the finger the real trophy? Or was the act of getting the ball what mattered? Or the desire itself? Or the willingness to throw the ball away? Or were they telling me that a grail lost its power once you possessed it? At some point I'd decided that all they'd been able to tell me was that Charlie Mexico was just another crazy, delirious friend of my father's, intoxicated by speed and fistfights and Stroh's.

But sitting there at the kitchen table in my home three decades later, when I was older than either of them had been that day, and with the manifestation of my own insane battle on the plate in front of me, I wasn't so sure that the baseball itself hadn't been the most valuable thing in Charlie Mexico's life.

Sitting on the couch, I reached across the valley created by the border of our legs, and touched my index finger to a pale patch on the tip of Beth's nose that you could only see if you knew to look for it. Almost twenty years ago, she'd torn off a chunk of skin with a fingernail while batting at a paper airplane a friend of ours had thrown at her. She also had a nearly invisible scar at the bottom of her right eyebrow, where her younger brother had thrown a burnt brownie at her when they were kids. And, on the ball of her left foot, a mysterious, tiny hard spot that had been there since I'd known her.

I said, "What I was trying to tell you earlier is that I figured out something really important today."

"How to sprint?"

"That too," I said. I dropped my hand from her cheek and wrapped my fingers around hers. "I'm sticky."

She pulled her hands away, flipped them over, and examined her fingers.

I waggled my hands in front of Beth's face and said, "Not sticky like that. You know—bike sticky."

"Oh," Beth said.

There are all kinds of bike riders, with names passed down from their original French, Belgian, Italian, and generally legendary origins. There are the roleurs, tough cyclists who can turn the pedals over at high speeds for miles and miles, without cracking. There are the grimpeurs, the angels of the mountains, who fly up leg-breaking slopes. There are flahutes, who excel in mud and cobbles and cold. There are domestiques, whose sole job is to protect their leaders. Rarest of all are the campionissimo, the champions among champions—the immortals. I was the least glorious, least noble, silliest-named bicycle racer of all. I was sticky. My only talent on a bike: I was hard to get rid of. Always there, never first, other cyclists said of the sticky. Great teammates. Terrible leaders. We were tenacious failures.

"But," said Beth, "you knew that."

It was true. My stickiness was no revelation. All of us knew what kind of riders the others were. Beth was a rhythm climber.

"Yeah," I said. "But—I mean, I'm sticky. I mean, in life." I put both my arms over her collarbones and pulled her toward me. We dropped our chins over each other's shoulders, then I pulled my head back and nuzzled into the space between her neck and the fine curve of her collarbone. "That's all I have," I said.

Beth didn't say anything. She slid two fingers into my hair. I listened to her breathe. I said, "It means I'm not a winner."

"Oh come on," said Beth. Her fingers tickled their way down my head, onto my shoulder. "You scored—"

"No," I said. "I know this now. And it's a good thing. I used to think it was a weakness. I mean, it is a weakness—a big one—but it's also my strength." I raised my head up and looked into her green eyes from a distance of two inches. Our noses brushed. "I'm not built to win. I'm built to not lose. I'm going to—I'm going to screw stuff up, you know, my whole life, and I'm never going to quite ever get what I want. Or be able to give you everything you deserve." I took her hands again, and shook them once, up and down, as if we were agreeing on something. "But I'm sticky, see, so no matter what happens I don't lose—not everything, anyway, which is what I've been afraid of my whole life."

The refrigerator hummed. A bug flew against a window. Outside the front door, Jasper meowed to be let in. Beth and I breathed against each other.

After a while, she leaned away from me and laid a palm flat against my chest. She pushed me backward and said, "I'll show you sticky."

twenty-two

AND I REALLY WAS DIFFERENT. I COULD FEEL WITHIN me the coiled poise of a pure cyclist. My body was suffused with a whispering, tensile certainty that scoring more points would be easy. It was.

Beth and Natalie had met me in the parking lot before the Crit, with the bag of Cheese Curls. I took the orange stick Natalie handed me, saving it to crunch at the start line, where three or four people around me snickered. When the race began, I floated in it, stripped of thought, naked of everything about me that was not a bike racer, nearly drowsy in the warmth of our momentum. The breathy roar of the pack ran under my wheels. The single-file line we became curved from one edge of the asphalt to the other, as stirring as the brush-stroke of a great artist. I rode my bicycle, the simplest yet most comprehensive description of me at that moment. That was all that I was doing. The feel I had for the race was like that of someone who had put their hand on a stereo speaker for the first time and discovered that music could not only be listened to, but touched. Bells knelled, but not for me. Somewhere in there one of the bells was mine, and I opened myself to absorb the suffering of the pack, rising up and over the hill into blurriness, then blankness. My wheels sang that strange knifing music of speed, and I became aware of other bikes beside me, then falling back, and at the line I was third, gaining fast on second and first.

Two points.

I eased off the pedals. The pack washed around me. Recovery was the hardest part of racing. In contrast to immolating your body in a sprint or a chase, simply trying to hang on after one of those efforts was a slow undertaking that demanded not the glorious scaling of a peak but the grim tenacity to stay out of the valley, to summon the focus ninety times in a single minute to not ease off on one pedal stroke. My entire ambition had to be marshaled and spent on each revolution of each foot, with no grand treasure such as a point awaiting me, no reward except the gift of being able to keep doing this to myself. And though it felt like life or death, of course it was not.

To stop, all you had to do was stop. The same mind that generated that thought implored me to ignore it. Things ripped loose inside me that I had spent a year building for the sole purpose of being able to rip them loose. I spit my breaths out. I drifted back, in love with the sport of cycling. I noticed that I was beside one of those racers I'd made friends with during my apprenticeship of belonging, a big barrel of a woman. Neither of us knew the other's name.

She said, "Am I scaring you?"

"No," I said. I didn't know what she meant.

"Did I seem squirrelly?"

I looked at her kind of sideways, keeping my left eye on the bikes in front of us, and I said, "No." I spit onto my thigh. "No more squirrelly than that sprint of mine."

"Which one?"

"The one that just happened," I said. "I could barely see, but I ended up getting two points."

She looked hard at me, squinting. Frowning.

"What?" I said. "I scored, right?"

"That was like seven laps ago," she said.

I concentrated on breathing. I concentrated on not looking for a memory of the last seven laps.

"Just now," she said, "before you came back here that guy in black and blue swerved in front of me and I almost hit him, and I think I overreacted and looked squirrelly."

"What lap is this?" I asked.

"There are fourteen left," she said, and just then, sure enough, we went by the finish and the counter said fourteen. "So this is lap sixteen," she said.

"I don't think you're squirrelly," I said. "You're not squirrelly at all compared to me." I had an impulse to confess that I had deliberately caused a crash back in June. But before my mouth could open, I stood up on the pedals and swung out beside the pack and sprinted to the front, where I slotted in next to a guy called Pickle. That was a fast nickname.

"You ever black out during a race?" I asked.

"You ever not black out?" he asked, and he attacked up the

side, and I followed him, and I passed him on the hill and he passed me back, inside, the two of us bumping arms and elbows like a couple of kids wrestling because they couldn't sit still, and already I could not wait for the next Crit.

twenty-three

THE NEXT MORNING AS WE WERE ALL GETTING READY, bustling around the house to butter pancakes and fill Tigger's bowl, to brush our hair and find our shoes and think about what it meant to score two more points, Beth and I collided in the kitchen. Natalie was sitting at the table over by the big, sunny bay window, eating. Beth waggled her finger at me: Come here.

I followed her down the hall. She stopped in front of Nat's room and said, "You have to see this. Did you see this?" I shook my head no, and we went in.

Beth walked to Natalie's bookshelf, picked up the dream box, and held it out to me. I lifted the lid off. There was a dense crumple of paper lodged inside. I turned the box over and shook it against my palm, but the paper wouldn't come out, so I dug at it with my finger until it popped free. It was folded crooked, four and a half times, and as I exposed its center I could see pink letters written in Natalie's five-year-old script: "I wish I could fly."

"Holy shit," I said, backing into Natalie's dresser as I looked at Beth, who shrugged her shoulders. "Now what?"

Beth said, "She believes in dreams. She really does."

"That's great—that's perfect. All we have to do to keep that alive is invent the power of human flight."

Both of us knew that, just as a stuffed cat technically fit the criteria of our daughter's kitten wish but would have been all wrong, there was no way this wish could be fulfilled by giving her a ride in a helicopter, or by taking her to the clouds in a hot-air balloon, or even by helping her get a pilot's license when she was old enough. She expected to be granted the ability to fly under her own power.

Beth, who'd laughed at my outburst, said, "Look, the important thing is that we made her kitten wish come true. And you're going to make her ten points wish come true. That's two out of three. That's better than a lot of people get their whole lives."

I stood there, holding the paper in my hand, my butt perched on the top of Natalie's dresser. Were two answered dreams enough—whatever enough was, and whatever enough was for? Would my ten points be enough? Are you a fool if you sell orange Melmac for $8 or if you buy it for $100? At the end of his life, whenever and however that had come, had throwing the baseball from the car still been worth more to Charlie Mexico than having it?

Beth took the paper from my hand and began refolding it. "Don't say anything to her," she said as she stuffed Natalie's wish back into the box and closed the lid. "She didn't tell me.

I saw the box sitting there on her desk instead of her dresser, and opened it."

Out in the hall, alone, I stopped in front of the papyrus scroll. I put my index finger against the cool glass, covering the face of the crocodile god who stood patiently waiting to eat the heavy-hearted dead. You didn't avoid the horror just by making your heart as light as a feather; you had to keep it that way.

I stretched out my shower that morning, shaving my face and my legs, which I almost never did on the same day. Beth poked her head through the steam, leaned into the streaming water, and kissed me, then said she was taking Nat to pre-K. When I was done and dressed and alone, I opened the top drawer of Beth's nightstand and began looking for an envelope I knew she kept in there.

Two years earlier, Valentine's Day had come as Beth and I were still fighting to save our marriage, just four months after my infidelity had been revealed. The idea of buying Beth a box of chocolates felt insincere, flowers like a kind of mockery. I wanted an expression of the visceral love that, it seemed, day by day could equally elude or assault us, as if we were hunting a mouse we could hear scratching around in the walls of our home, only to end up wrestling a bear in our living room. In tiny letters, I typed out a long list of things I loved about Beth, things that made me think of her, things that made her different. I scissored each thought into its own strip of paper—little confetti thoughts, a quarter of an inch tall and no more than two or three inches long. I scattered them around the house, some in obvious places she'd find when she woke on Valentine's Day—the drawer where she'd reach for our toothpaste, in the cabinet on top of her overturned coffee cup, on our telephone cradle—and others for future discovery, on the keyboard of her computer, under the butter dish, inside a book I knew she planned to read, in the pocket of the jacket she wouldn't use until spring.

"That afternoon of sledding in the woods . . . That pop your toe made when I gave you therapy after your foot surgery . . . How you do all the different voices when you tell a story . . . You washed my hair when I had a broken leg . . . Ham and baby Swiss sandwiches on our college road trips . . . When you're straddling me and your hair hangs in front of your face . . ."

Beth had been puzzled when she found the first few, scrunching her eyes there in the bathroom. Then she'd been surprised when she kept finding them that morning. By that evening, her face had taken on a warm, almost blushing shyness. "How many of these are there?" she'd asked, holding a handful, leaning in to give me a kiss without waiting for an answer.

She'd kept finding one or two a day for the next few weeks when she'd move a dish or pull out the rag she cleaned windows with, or needed to wear her red shoes. "Old photos of you in tube socks . . . Thinking of you reading these . . . Your face when nobody but me understood you weren't afraid to do scuba but couldn't get the breathing . . . That every morning you still tell me what you dreamed . . . That funny, cartoony time you slipped on the ice on the porch in Cincinnati and the door banged you in the head . . . How your calf muscles look in that snapshot from the Cascades . . ."

Over the next few months, she still discovered one or two

strips a week. If I was around, she'd bring it out to me, smiling, flattered all over again. When I wasn't there, she'd add it to the envelope she collected them in, sometimes remembering to tell me that night that she'd found a new one, but sometimes only remembering a few days later, when something reminded her. By the next Valentine's Day, she hadn't found one of those strips for months, and flowers felt right again.

One afternoon last winter, Beth walked over to where I was sitting in the living room and dropped a fluttering strip of paper into my lap. I picked it up and read: "You remember everyone's birthday."

I looked up at her. Her eyes were bright. "Well," I said, "the paper doesn't lie. You do."

"I'm going to find these forever, aren't I?"

"Where was this one?"

"Stuck to the back of the vegetable crisper. I was cleaning the refrigerator—it's disgusting—and pulled the drawer out to scrub it."

"I didn't hide any back there. I don't think. It must have fallen down back behind the shelves."

"So, really," she said. "How many did you make?"

"I don't know. A hundred. Hundreds."

It hadn't been Natalie's doomed wish that made me think of these declarations of love, but the insatiable crocodile god. I shook the strips out onto the bedspread and began to read some. "Your vegetable soup . . . Your beautiful, full, firm, lean ass . . . The incredible detail when you recount an anecdote . . . The time those people thought we were having sex in the elevator . . . The funny guy who drove us to our wedding . . . The lemonade ice we ate on our wedding day . . . How you look in black . . ." I'd forgotten how small each statement was. They stuck to my fingertips, and adhered to each other through static attraction, refusing to be separated or flipped over. I really had no idea how many I'd made. I'd forgotten many that I read. "The salty taste of your back after you work in your garden . . . My fingers in your hair while I sleep . . ." I remembered writing one that I hadn't seen yet. I flipped through the pile looking for it.

"The tilt of your nose . . . That you cooked up Nat in your belly . . . Your baby pictures . . . Finding notes you wrote me in the eighties . . . You in jeans and tennis shoes . . . Your brownie scar . . . The picture of you practicing 'And Now Good Morrow' on our wedding morning . . ."

It wasn't there. It was still out there somewhere in our home, waiting to remind Beth of the first wish she had granted this family. Although now it was a fact, at the time I'd written it neither of us could have known if it was anything more than a hope. It said: You saved me.

twenty-four

BETH CALLED TO REMIND ME THAT BECAUSE THE BAG OF Cheese Curls hadn't made it through our second celebration, and because there was no way Nat was going to show up at the Crit without the magic snack food, they were going to stop at the convenience store on their way.

"Great," I said, trapping my phone between my ear and my shoulder as I used both hands to smooth my jersey out on the ticking, still-hot hood of my truck.

"Hey."

"Yeah?"

"I love you."

"I'd love it if I could learn how to pin my number on," I said. "Four points—and I still look like a beginner every week."

"We love you anyway," said Beth, and hung up.

The pinning of the plasticized paper rectangle was an intricate task. It had to be fastened so the judges could easily decipher it amid a knot of riders flying by at nearly 40 mph—half on my back and half on my left side, slanted for style in a way that suggested jauntiness yet still rendered the three big, bold, black digits set starkly against white. If the judges missed a number, claimed Steak, who frequently lurked near the finish line like the conscience of a lost man, they sometimes simply assigned the unidentified racer's place in the sprint to someone they were able to recognize. (Among his season's collection of finish-line horror stories, including the squirrel that nearly brought down the pack and the sprint decided by a thrown water bottle, there was the tale of the hungry judge, the mis-flip of the lap counter, and the verdict to "just give the points to four of the guys who always score.")

Some weeks I would pin the number too low on my side, where it caught wind and flapped incessantly, costing me some infinitesimal extra amount of energy that, by the time I finished calculating its toll throughout an entire race, exacted an immense and nearly unsurvivable psychic cost. What's more, the number had to be crumpled to show everyone it was not new, yet it had to lay flat. An overly ripply number was like a topographic map of inexperience—the higher and more numerous the peaks, the less a racer knew. To achieve a flat lie, the number had to be pulled taut at the corners, but not so excessively hyperextended that it might rip free of the safety pin when the jersey expanded as I pulled it on.

Despite these travails while pinning, I had to project a casual, nearly bored ease, because fussing with the number was a more grievous transgression than sloppy placement. I allowed myself two re-pins, for a maximum of six insertions of my four safety pins. Some racers stuck additional pins along each side between the corners, or sometimes even two between each corner, for up to twelve pins in all, but as with any detectable weakness, the penchant for fastidiousness that was manifested by engineering such a flat, flutter-proof number was used against those racers at crucial times. I did keep a secret fifth pin in my backpack in case I dropped one on the pavement. I could not take the chance of being witnessed stooping for one I'd fumbled.

I had three pins in to my satisfaction when Ray coasted past my truck. Pivoting in his saddle to face me as he rolled away, he said, "Five minutes, Strickland."

"What?" I yelled.

"Five ticks to the gun."

I shook my head. He had the time wrong. "Thirty minutes," I said. I hadn't even warmed up.

Ray cut a tight half-circle and, as he rolled back around me, said, "The start time was moved up because it's getting too dark at the finish."

Chip was beginning his pre-race speech when I cut through the back of the pack and, as was my right now that I was known as one who could score, nosed into the fourth row—albeit with a fluttery number. Ray and the Animal were in front of me. Beside me was Ken, who, after battling out a tough season in the early race, had made it into the Crit. Although we'd been unable to race together, the two of us had spent more than a hundred hours on training rides. He and I didn't have much in common. He went to church regularly. He was some kind of engineer, built lasers or computer chips or something I couldn't understand, had a doctorate, and knew a lot about a lot, but was soft-spoken. Naturally gifted as an athlete, he would have been one of the best, even in this pack, if he rode as much as I did. Even at his current, relatively untrained level, he could sometimes ride with the strongest packs, and when he did he'd say stuff like, "It sure is neat to be able to stay with the leaders." Sometimes after a ride, when I was at his house and in response to a question I said something like, "Shit, yeah," I'd feel as if I'd just spilled a drink or knocked something over in his densely decorated living room. The only thing we really had in common was bikes, but that was a lot to have in common. It was the atmosphere and ground of our friendship. Since I'd gotten to know him, there had been a few times when I'd wanted to ask him if someone like him—a normal, great guy, with an important job and a pretty wife and a cute daughter Natalie's age—ever felt like I did almost every day, as if you had to concentrate your entire being on hanging on, on staying sticky, not to win but just to avoid losing everything. When I wanted to ask him that, I would say "Want to climb this hill?" or "Let's clean the road," and off we would go.

Standing there waiting for the start, Ken said, "If I have the legs, let me work for you."

"I don't know," I said. There were only two races left, and I needed six points. So far, I'd been able only once per race to muster the insane amount of energy I needed for a top four. To get my six points, I'd need to either finish second or higher in a sprint in both of the last two races, or get points in more than one sprint per race. Yet, all season, it had been important to me, for a reason I could accept but not understand, to ride the Crit unattached, with no prearranged favors. I didn't shun the informal and ephemeral alliances that formed while we

214

rode—that was part of the race, one of the inevitabilities of belonging to the pack. But I felt that I couldn't achieve what I needed to if I had teammates to drag me into breaks, to shield me from the wind at key moments, to tow me to the pack when I popped, to pull me to the front of the sprints then swing away when the line was at my nose. I'd probably have scored more than the four points I had, perhaps even ten already. But those points would not have given me what I needed.

"I got to score on my own," I said.

The Animal heard me and turned around. "You've been taking some points," he said.

"Some," I said. "Almost enough. I'm shooting for ten this season."

The Animal nodded, as if I'd picked the right number, and then his chin in a series of upward spirals tipped skyward and he seemed to open his nostrils, sampling the air. He snapped his head back down and said, "Sneaky wind tonight."

That meant an early scuffle. "Thanks," I said.

We missed the break. The Animal and Elliston and Speedy and three or four others had started by sitting on the pack, forcing us into a creep that tempted all the riders from the rear to swarm forward. Because the pack was slow, the back-of-the-packers felt fast. This must have seemed like the chance for which they'd ridden the whole cruel season, the moment that was going to make every second of suffering and humiliation worthwhile. They infested the asphalt from side to side, flitting and buzzing against us, and just as they consumed the last of the open road, the Animal lunged forward and away, a brutal burst that snapped off the pack behind him. The head-wind rushed into the gap, the weak riders smashed against it, and the pack nearly ran over itself.

Brakes squealed. Tires shed rubber against the pavement. Voices cursed, blamed, cried out. From far behind came the scrape of metal on pavement. Ray bulled forward, sending riders bobbling out away from him as if he were a big rock dropped in a pond. Bird got his wheel, broadened his shoulders, and opened a breach that Ken poured into and then me. As the hole began crashing in around me, I slipped a hitch into my stroke to hesitate a quarter-second and braced my elbows against the collapsing wall of bike racers, hoping at least one more strong rider would come through behind me. Then I had to go before I lost Ken's wheel. I didn't have time to see if we'd dragged any help along.

We could see the break, already thirty feet clear, working like some kind of assembly line that whipped bicycle racers along a conveyor belt for a brief turn at the front before shut-tling them back to be refilled with energy. At the front, each rider took five- or ten-stroke pulls, nearly the shortest you'd ever use, which meant they were at max.

The Animal snuck a look back as my group cleared the dis-integrating pack. There was Ray up front, and me, then Ken and Bird, and Bleachy Blonde Foreign Champion Chick and Clove, who was trailing a tail of three or four riders who looked sick just getting this far. The race was no longer thirty laps. It was the 30 feet between us and the attack. If we couldn't catch them, we'd never score.

Ray dumped himself into his pedals. He was punching his body through the headwind at 32 mph, and I knew it had to be leg-breaking. I couldn't wait for my chance. It came in twenty pedal strokes. Gears sang, wheels whooped, and I was done with my twenty. We worked, and hurt, and shuffled back, and recovered, and waited for the race to strip us down to where we needed to be, to the place where we would be only and purely riding.

The Animal's group stayed 30 feet in front of us for a few laps, stretched the gap out to 50 or 60 feet, then came back, but never any closer than the original 30 feet. There was no reason for them to waste energy riding faster than us. All they had to do was maintain their gap, rocking their efforts back and forth to match ours, until we blew up.

We coughed and spat and grunted and took turns, and chased and gained nothing.

No thing.

No points.

I was at my best when I was about to lose.

The Animal looked back to gauge the gap and adjust his group's speed, and I remembered something he'd said to me once during those two months when I found my way into the pack. He'd just recovered from leading a single-file, two-lap chase that had failed to catch a breakaway but ended up costing the escaped riders so much energy that they'd blown apart moments after the Animal had. "Sometimes if you can't catch them," he'd said, "you can crack them."

Ray pulled off.

I sloped down over my bike, stretched my hands out over the brake hoods, scooted as far back on the saddle as I could, and began to bury myself.

I was a magnificent piece of work, the art of sinew and muscle and blood birthed from a season full of sacrifice, and for a few moments as I scooped away the pavement in front of us I had a narcissist's appreciation of the functioning of my own body. I could not merely pedal a bicycle faster than most people alive, but in absolute numbers I was on that Thursday night easily in the top 1 percent of all of humanity ever when it came to propelling this strange toy. The moment stretched out behind and in front of me, and the awareness of the effort it took to maintain maximum speed straight into the wind piled onto me, thickening, deepening as it stretched wider around me. I chased through the haze, then climbed down into the hole of my effort and pulled the earth shut over me, six feet deep in the euphoria of self-destruction and, finally, the bicycle and I were nothing.

And the gap began closing.

I continued my pull, only intermittently and vaguely aware I was in a bicycle race, the way you might notice the sun on a partly cloudy day. I could feel the chain of my friends tugging on me as if I were actually dragging them along the road. I was glad for the resistance because I began to fear that if I were to become untethered from them I would go shooting off down the road, accelerating until I caught on fire and began disintegrating, tumbling end over crumbly end until I dispersed into ashes.

The gap closed to 10 feet.

But, of course, the five people ahead of us were even more magnificent pieces of work. They were the top 1 percent of the top 1 percent, national class, world class, pro level. Inside their bodies, mitochondria fired off with more rapidity and force than mine ever could. Their lungs sucked in amounts of air that, in my body, would have made me feel as if I were drowning in oxygen. With each pump of their hearts, the blood traveled farther and faster, and carried more payload than mine. Noticing that their lead in the race was shrinking, they took a few seconds to stretch the kinks out of their legs and backs, wiggled around a bit on their saddles to get comfortable, then unleashed their bodies onto the course and rode away from us. Their pedals spun. They became not a pack but a sliver ahead of us that flickered, then faded to translucence, nothing more than a wavery vertical disturbance at the meeting of pavement and sky, something you were not even sure you saw.

I was going to pop. I could feel it rising in me, a kind of bubble that quivered each time it was jostled by one of my pedal strokes. I pulled off to the right and tried to hold my body still. The line had reshuffled during my pull. The strongest riders had swept around to fill gaps as people faltered, and Ray had ended up on my wheel. I didn't look at him but I could sense by the leonine stance of his body as he passed that he was going to make a run that was faster and more fierce than mine. The line of chasers rumbled by me, down to three. I let them go.

I looked back and saw racers from my group and the remnants of the main pack scattered all across the course. For a while I watched Ray. He might someday become one of those magnificent bike racers, but he wasn't one today and he wasn't going to catch them today. No one was going to catch the true monsters of the pack. They'd set themselves free, flying across the asphalt with an ease of motion that made it difficult to tell if they spun over the Earth or the Earth spun under them, beautiful, glorious creatures molded from the speed and suffering they made within themselves.

My race was over. I shivered. I coasted. I shifted into my easiest gear and dragged my feet around the circles inscribed by my pedals, and as I approached the finish line alone, I saw Beth and Natalie and Steak.

Steak was holding out a Cheese Curl.

twenty-five

"DADDY. YOU DIDN'T GET A CHEESE CURL," SAID Natalie.

I was straddling my bike at the finish line, my forearms draped over the handlebar, my head hanging down onto them. My eyes were closed.

"Daddy," Natalie said again. "You didn't get a Cheese Curl."

I shook my head, rolling it back and forth on my arms.

"No," I whispered.

"Did you get points?"

I raised my head and, without focusing, stared at Natalie, standing just in front of my bike. "No points, beautiful girl," I said, my voice a croak. I reached out and touched her head. "I got popped." As if to illustrate my statement, the lead group whistled past in a points sprint. Beth put her arm across my shoulder. Steak, pretending to watch the race, drifted away a few steps.

As Natalie and I walked the bike to the truck, each on our customary side, each with one hand on the handlebar, I said, "I only have one race left, Nat."

We walked. She stared ahead.

I said, "I don't think I can score six points in one race."

We walked. I said, "What I'm saying is that I might not get ten points."

"Daddy?" Natalie's voice was strained, trembling. When I looked over at her, across the bike, her eyes had grown enormous, and wet. "I'm sorry I was too late to give you a Cheese Curl."

She bawled.

I couldn't breathe. I was immediately full of regret for how selfish I'd been. I switched my left hand to the bar, then reached over the frame with my right, wrapped my arm around Natalie's back, and lifted her up and over the bike. I brought her against me. I kissed her forehead. I took my left hand from the bike, letting it lean against us, and I wiped her face. Then I wrapped both arms around her and hugged as if I could squeeze the misplaced weight of my loss out of her.

She cried more, harder, her chest punching out at mine. I searched for something to tell her. I didn't even know what to tell myself about the death of ten points. It was too fresh, yet had run too deep—like a flash flood that would drown a weak sentiment such as "It's not your fault." I stood mute in the parking lot while my daughter wailed out her guilt over a dream I maybe never should have had. Her emotion was so irrational, yet so intricately woven into her life that I was unprepared to extract it. For all the good I was, it might as well have been not her metaphorical heart but the real thing that needed repair; I not only had no idea where to start, I was sure anything I tried would only worsen the situation.

The wind blew, a late-day October wind, and it carried over to us the sound of the jangling bell, a muffled chorus of shouts. Involuntarily, I turned my head from Natalie to see if I could get a glimpse of the pack flying over the hill. Across the parking lot, over a green field, halfway to the hill, the race streamed by. When I swiveled my head back to Nat, her eyes, just inches from mine, were looking out at the race course too. She was quiet.

"It's only points, Nutto," I said and gave her a soft bounce with the crook of my left arm. She kept looking at the race course. I began walking, holding her against me with my left arm while with the other guiding the bicycle by its saddle. "One day, when I was little younger than you," I said, "I was riding in a car with my daddy and his good friend Charlie Mexico." And, minus the drunkenness, and the 100-mph speed, and the goriest details of the broken finger—although I kept the finger in to illustrate consequence and worth—I told her the story of Charlie Mexico's baseball.

We had been standing at the truck for a while when I finished.

"So, see, the baseball didn't matter," I concluded. "It's like the Cheese Curl."

"Daddy. That does not make sense."

"Yeah—maybe not. What was important was not the baseball, but the idea that Charlie Mexico wanted the baseball so much that he was willing to break his finger. Like, the Cheese Curls aren't—I mean, they're—I mean what was important is that you wanted to give me one."

"Why did he throw the baseball out of the car?"

"I've never really been sure," I admitted. I helped her up onto the bumper, and she lifted a leg over the tailgate and began climbing in. I said, "I think maybe magic isn't in a baseball, or a Cheese Curl, or even Bella. I think the point is—I think it's the same thing the pack taught me once—that we decide. You, and me, and Mommy, we all kind of get to decide what we are, if we are point scorers or pack fodder, or if we're going to throw our baseball out, or if we're going to have faith, Boo, or even if we're going to do crazy—"

She was twirling circles in the bed of truck, not really listening to me, for which, at least this one time, I was glad. "Crazy shit like if we'll pull a trigger," I said aloud, finishing the sentence, but so only I could hear. Then, louder: "Nat? We're going to go on wishing for things and working hard for things and trying to get things all our lives, and we're going to do it together. Sometimes we'll make magic and sometimes we won't. And what matters is not whether or not I eat a Cheese Curl, but that you wanted me to get ten points and I wanted to get them for you so much that we ended up believing in a Cheese Curl. That's it."

Natalie was standing motionless in the truck bed, looking down at me. She said, "I would never throw Bella out of a car."

"No."

This would have been a failure, except that, whether she'd forgiven herself, or forgotten what we were originally talking about, or simply been confused by my babbling, Natalie seemed to have shed her guilt.

"That was a funny story, Daddy," she said. "About the baseball."

"Yeah?" I'd never thought of it that way.

"Tell me another funny story."

"How about the time my mom saw me eating ants off the sidewalk?"

"About your daddy," she said.

"Not now," I said. "How about when my dog ate a pickle?"

"About your daddy. Tell me a funny story about him while we drive home." She walked across the bed of the truck and put her hand on the cab window, preparing to slide it open so she could climb in. "Please?" Natalie hesitated, her hand flat on the glass. It struck me that, just as with my father and me, Natalie knew almost nothing about her grandfather, what he looked like or what he'd done for a living or where he was from. She knew that he was dead.

From far away came the pealing of the sprint bell. I took a breath. I said, "Once, my dad believed I could outrace a poodle."

I'd stepped on a honeybee again.

My body was never going to let me get a chance to outrun the pack. For two weeks I'd been soaring in a brilliant state of peak fitness, floating far above what I'd imagined was my highest capacity for performance. Now, the blazing level I'd achieved was melting my wings and I'd tip down into what would be a long, screaming descent. I'd gone through this cycle, as all racers did, three or four times throughout the season. Each time you climbed back up higher. Each time you plunged lower.

I should have seen it coming. But you never knew the bee was there until you stepped on it.

The phrase had survived as an inside joke between my father and me, the one thing from the worst part of my life to emerge intact—and the sole memory of his insanity, that my father could still bring into the open after he'd left the dining room and put the gun back in the closet and, as suddenly as if I'd graduated from some kind of twisted tutelage, stopped making me eat shit, stopped beating me and shooting my dogs, and tried his best to be an ordinary father.

When I ran the car out of gas while ditching high school and called him for help, the first thing he said when he showed up was, "You stepped on a bee." And when I called him on the phone to borrow fifty bucks so I could finally buy an English textbook the week before finals, he said, "Yeah, we don't want you stepping on any bees." When I stood over his coffin and looked in at him, and I thought of how we'd come to a restless peace but never any kind of resolution, I thought, "You stepped on the bee. Why'd you step on the bee?"

I had that phrase and an old hockey shirt from my father. Plus whatever it was he'd put into me, the result of what I'd come to think of as the exclusive trial of my soul. Throughout our childhoods, my sister Leann accumulated twenty-one stitches in her head, but I'd been in the room the day she fell off the bed and cracked her skull on the rail, and I'd been there when she'd gotten caught in the fray of our front-yard football game. I'd seen my father hitting my mother exactly once, and she'd been kicking his ass when I opened the door to their bedroom to find out what all the noise was about. She was pinned underneath him on the floor, but clearly in charge, thonking a thick glass vase off the top of his head over and over. She'd paused when she saw me, screamed "Get out of here!", and resumed her barrage. I'd backed out of the room and closed the door. As I'd grown up, I'd gradually accepted and even become in a way proud of what my father had told me—that he'd been teaching me to be a Strickland, me alone, because some chosen few among us harbored a curse, a defect, a demon that we would not be able to endure without extraordinary lessons.

With my body returning to its normal state, I felt foolish that I'd imagined I could use a bicycle to destroy an elemental part of who I was. I could no more use my pedals to crush the curse of myself than I could use them to chase down the Animal. But even though I would have to go on living as I had before, with the core emotions of my life carefully registered for signs of danger, I would no longer live in fear, thanks to the pack. Although I could not win the death of the curse inside me, I knew now that I would never lose to it my life, my wife, my daughter. The pack had taught me how to be sticky.

Just as I was falling asleep that night, Beth whispered, "Bill." She rolled to her side, put an arm over me, and spoke into my ear. "When I went into Natalie's room, I saw the paper with her flying wish on the floor. I asked her what it was for."

"What'd she say?"

"She wouldn't look at me. You know how she gets embarrassed? So I asked her again and she said, 'I just wrote that down in case I needed it sometime.'"

"Did she tell you it used to be in the dream box?"

"No. Do you think she gave up on a wish?"

"I don't know," I said.

"Do you think you can score six points next week?"

We lay there for a long time. I imagined all the miraculous outcomes I could, and when none of them was enough, I said, "No."

twenty-six

But I'd forgotten one mundane miracle: Rain. The mist that fell over us while we stood hushed at the start line of the last Thursday Night Crit of the season was perfect—just enough to make the course slippery, but not quite enough to force a cancellation. I stood there in line with my face raised to the falling water, the thing that always transformed me into one of the best racers of the pack, the only thing in the world that might offset the decline of my body. I'd barely been able to turn my pedals around on lunch-time rides and, in mid-week, finally just gave up on the idea of training and took two days off before the Crit. From far above, liquid fell to anoint me—whether through foolhardiness, or luck, or my affinity for being at my best when things were at their worst, or perhaps a single incongruous strand of world-class skill in my mediocre genetics—capable of scoring six points.

Ken, a man who on a bicycle possessed immeasurably more potential than me for inflicting pain, leaned over and said, "It's slick out there, but if I can keep up with you, I'm helping you get your points. No matter what the heck you say." I smiled at him, at his language, at the white cotton tube socks he wore instead of fancy, synthetic cycling socks. This nice guy had become my friend, against all odds, and at an age when we're not supposed to make any more friends.

"You fucking got it," I said as the whistle blew.

Throughout the first two laps, as the pack sloshed across the pavement, all of us dragging our brakes far in advance of every corner to squeegee water off the rims of our wheels, something warm was spreading upward through my body, from my stomach to my shoulders: anticipation. We heard the bell for the first sprint and I waited, savoring the lull as we toddled through the oily corners and wriggled up the hill. Then I attacked.

Into the mist and muck and grit, I sped off, disappearing into the dark of the woods, sliding through its corners, and coming out of the last turn onto the straightaway before the finish line clear of everyone. There was nothing between me and the five points awarded for first except 60 feet, a distance that in my hardest gear I would cover in less than two full pedal strokes, a motion that at this speed, 37 mph, I would complete in about one second.

In that one second, four people passed me.

One of them was Elliston. The other three were muted blurry colors hard on his wheel, whipping their heads in panic to shake off the dark spew driven into their faces by the roostertail that sprayed off Elliston's wheel, higher than his head.

I'd lost the sprint, gone from five points to zero in the span of two pedal strokes.

I had to catch the move. I wrenched my bike back and forth. The chain hissed. One of the riders on Elliston cracked off, coming at me so fast it looked like he was sprinting backward. I dodged around him and, still out of the saddle, screamed and rode within fifteen feet of Elliston's break.

I gained on them in every corner, skating my wheels across the fine layer of water that lay over the track, riding on liquid rather than asphalt. Twice as I turned, my bike fell out from under me and I banged a pedal against the pavement.

But every time the course straightened, Elliston was clearly riding his group away from me. In this pattern I kept tempo, falling then rising, but never changing. I looked behind me for the pack. There was no pack. Cyclists smudged the track here and there, muddied jerseys and darkened helmets held down and forward like shields against the rain and wind. Just as I turned my head forward, I saw one spot of color streaking up along the course, gathering the bent helmets behind it as it came, growing the tail that strong riders always sprouted as they moved through a group.

It was Ken.

"Get on my wheel," he said when he rode up beside me.

He'd collected a good pack. There was one of the fast kids, a couple guys who'd scored a point or two through the season, and five or six others who knew how to chase. Ken pulled at the front while we slotted into single file, then he pulled a little more to set the rhythm and to give us a sense of the timing he thought would work, then he swung off and came back. He didn't look at me when he drifted past. He was recovering.

We chased, swapping pulls and wiping our eyes clear. I rode conservatively in the corners to avoid cracking the chase apart, yet had to strain just to hang onto the pack in the straights. Elliston and the two guys on his wheel were always just in front of us, 30 feet, calibrating the gap.

When the sprint bell banged, Elliston's third rider snapped off and floated across the glistening pavement to us, not even trying to latch on as he sailed past. There were two. We chased across the line and through the curves and up and down the hill, and as we entered the slick, treacherous shadows of the woods, Ken came back from a pull and soft-pedaled when he reached my side. He said, "I'm going to pop myself to take you up to the break."

If Ken got me up there, all I had to do was hang behind Elliston for the remaining seven sprints. I'd get at least third—two points—every time, and maybe a second once or twice. I could have my six points in the next nine laps. I swung out of the paceline and fell in behind Ken.

This was it.

The season.

The curse.

The dream.

Ken jumped. I jumped.

And went nowhere.

Ken was up the side of our group, leaving me. He blasted past the lead rider. I jumped again. And went nowhere.

Ken was 5 feet clear of the pack. The kid sprang out of the front of our pack and caught Ken's wheel—the open wheel that had appeared in front of him like a miracle—and the two of them guzzled the pavement behind Elliston. I got out of

the saddle and sprinted, and watched Ken and the kid and Elliston and the rider who'd hung tough on his wheel roll away
from me.

I could see Natalie's bright red rain jacket beyond the finish
line. The white stripes of paint shone luminous off the asphalt. I
spun my legs faster, but went slower. It was as if every inhala-
tion sucked in not oxygen but wet concrete, a dense fatigue that
not only made me heavier but sloshed around inside me before
it settled. The fatigue hardened. I could feel it compressing my
organs, crushing me against my skin from the inside out.

I cracked. My body split into halves that, with each pedal
stroke, ground against each other like the two ends of a broken bone. Then I shattered into pieces that splashed and
pinged onto the watery course of the Thursday Night Crit
while my bike kept rolling along with something on it that
looked like me. When I realized the thing on my bike was me,
it was with a kind of calm acknowledgment, a remembrance of
something it seemed I'd long ignored, like rediscovering a
freckle on your shoulder. I had ridden the final hundred feet
to the finish line and was under the tree, behind the officials,
with Beth, and Natalie, and Ken, and Steak. Ray, who hadn't
raced this week, was there with his dog, a big goofy yellow
Lab. I was looking at Beth, and bringing my shoulders down
in the second half of a shrug. Because I did not want anyone
else to speak first or ask me anything—because Steak and Ken
and Beth and Natalie knew I wanted ten points but not why,
and Ray knew none of it—I said, "That was a hell of a finish."

Beth said, "That was a hell of a season, Bill."

"It was crazy out there," said Ken.

"Yeah," I said.

Steak put his hand on my shoulder.

"I popped so badly," Ken said.

"But he scored a point," said Ray, appraising Ken, a soft-spoken, middle-aged desk jockey who'd shown up and gotten a fourth in a sprint in the Thursday Night Crit.

Natalie said, "Daddy. I want to go home."

I shrugged Steak's hand off, clipped into my pedals, and rode around Ken, orbiting him. I said, "Thanks. For the help."

Ken tipped his chin up and put his gloved hand out, and I slapped it as I rode by him. He'd gotten a point. A point in the big race. I knew how that felt, remembered when I'd scored that sole point the previous season, when there was no point to a point except feeling good about it. I stuck my index finger up and wagged it at him and nodded, and he smiled a big, ex-hausted, popped, point-owning smile.

I circled my family and my friends old and new, and my beloved pack circled us, and I waited, as I once had for the wonderful suffering of racing, for the familiar sense of losing a dream to settle back into me, the acceptance of the unending vigilance the rest of my life would require.

Natalie said, "I am ready to be home."

I kept circling, waiting, but nothing came to me except a vague sense that I shouldn't ride away, that although I was about to lose, I was not yet at my best. I rode in circles.

Beth looked at me then said to Natalie, "I don't think Daddy's ready yet. I'll take you." She and Nat left the cover of the tree, walked to the edge of the racetrack, looked to make sure no riders were coming, then dashed off hand-in-hand through the rain. "Hang on!" yelled Beth as they ran.

Elliston and the kid and the third rider dopplered past us,

slipping and spinning, at least one of them nearly wiping out with every pedal stroke. I sat up. "Hey, Ray," I said. He looked over at me, and I said, "You remember that crash on the last lap in August?"

He shook his head no.

"It was my fault," I said. "I caused it. I did it. I crashed the pack."

"Strickland," he said, "shit happens."

I rode away, across the track and over the wet grass, onto the sidewalk, and into the parking lot. It started hot in my mouth and spread out across my face, cooking my head in the cool rain. It ran down into my chest and out through my arms, and settled infernal and sickening in my stomach. Shame.

Simple shame, that was all. That was the unbearable thing that had destroyed who knows how many generations of my family, an emotion that for some reason the first abused ancestor of mine must have found unendurable unless it was transformed into a grand curse, something that could be boasted about, that could be a source of twisted pride, that could be passed along like a sick heirloom. My childhood was not a curse, nor a destiny, just something shameful that happened to me a long time ago.

I stopped at the truck and unclipped. I got off my bike, holding myself up with one hand on the bar and the other on the saddle. Then I bent over, resting my head on my left arm. The rain of every shameful sin I'd ever committed or that had been committed upon me—from eating shit, to helping my father pull the trigger of a gun stuck in my mouth, to betraying my wife and failing to score ten points—fell hard on my back, and the monster was unmasked.

EPILOGUE

It is a chilly, bright spring afternoon, a Saturday in the year following that season of dreams, and Natalie and I have pedaled the tow-bike around our hill and up the other side, and we are poised at the peak, my bicycle already beginning to tilt down while hers still ascends.

"If you want to slow down," I say, "shout loud." I tuck my head and shoulders into a wedge and extend my arms to push the handlebar forward, tipping us fully into the descent. The road that plunges beneath us, beyond our sight, is one of the fastest miles in the Lehigh Valley. I have gone 51 mph on this drop. I have veered left across the double yellow line to blur past a school bus full of cheering elementary students.

"I'm afraid, Daddy," says Natalie as we begin to accumulate momentum. "But we have to go fast to fly." She is restating what I have told her, but she's also reassuring herself, her dream and her demon, like so many do, each finding its breath in the exhalation of the other.

"Faster," she urges. "Faster, Dadda."

Over the winter, the road has become spattered with potholes and gravel pools. Pebbles begin to spray up at our legs and crackle under our wheels, shifting beneath us like a floor in a carnival funhouse. The tow-bike shudders and yaws and begins yanking the rear of my bike from side to side. To stop this shimmy, we need to slow down, or accelerate through it into that mysterious state I momentarily inhabited in that Crit with Bobby Lea and Sarah Uhl, that ever-shifting point where the resonance of the road and the wind and our whirling wheels synchronize and all turbulence vanishes.

"Daddy!" screams Natalie.

"Tuck!" I yell back. "We'll ride through this."

Since last spring, Natalie has grown enough that I moved her saddle several inches higher, farther away from the wheel that grabbed her the day we wrecked. And I installed straps that will keep her feet from flying off the pedals. There's little danger of her falling off again, though I know it can't feel that way to her now. We'll crash only if I make a mistake. I squeeze my knees tight against the top tube of the bike. I pinch my shoulders together to narrow the projectile of my body even more, while lowering my head until my chin brushes the handlebar. I feel Natalie wiggle around and settle in. We gain speed but it's not enough. The bike convulses.

"Slower!" screams Natalie, and on each hand, two of my fingers reach out to the brake levers.

After the Crits, I began telling Beth, a little bit one day and a little bit a week later, and slowly all of it, what had happened to me. Then in a long, wrenching phone call, my mother and I talked about it. I ended up telling Steak and Jeremy and Ray a little, too, mostly on days when we got together to ride away the last precious weeks of the season.

Beth was sickened by some of the details, but not at all surprised. "There was something inside you," she said, plain and
accurate. Sometimes she held my head and stroked my hair.
Sometimes she cried with me or left me alone. Sometimes
she'd tell me the dishwasher needed emptying.

My mother wanted to cry, but wouldn't. For a long time as
we talked, she kept circling back to tear herself apart all over
again with the image of me wearing that special Reds cap the
day my father secretly broke my nose. That memory of me,
which for nearly four decades my mother had cherished as
one of those cute snapshots that inexplicably gain permanence
in our minds, had in a single phone call become a symbol of
her failure to protect me—an emblem for her, now, of everything that had gone wrong and how her strength and will,
which might have saved us all, had instead been focused on
keeping the family intact. Nearly two hours in, she said, "I
wish I'd pulled the trigger that night."

"What?"

"He used to beat me, Billy. On weekends. He'd come home
drunk and pass out, and when he woke up he'd beat me. I kept
quiet so you kids wouldn't hear." There was a long pause. I
could hear a bird chirping, singing, a parakeet—her only com-
panion in the one-room apartment she rents down in Florida.
"I tried not to make any noise, so you kids wouldn't know, so
you could have a normal life. But one night, Billy, I don't
know—I decided I couldn't take any more. When he passed
out, I took that gun from his closet and sat at the end of the
bed. When he woke up to beat me, I was going to kill him. But
your father was always so lucky. That was the one night he
didn't so much as stir."

The bird trilled and whistled, and my mother said, "I wish I'd pulled that trigger."

My sister, who lives just across town from my mother and has three kids, won't talk much about any of it. I'm no longer sure if I was there when she fell off the bed and busted her head open, or if I ran into the room while she was still lying on the floor screaming, which gives me an idea of what my mother must be enduring.

My friends would ask me hesitant questions, and sometimes they'd just stare at me. Once on a ride, trying to fill a post-confession silence that had gone on way too long, Jeremy said the first thing that came into his head: "That must have taught you a lot about courage."

"I was in sixth grade when my father stuck a gun in my mouth," I said. "I was eleven or twelve. That doesn't teach you about courage. It teaches you about fear."

I found out that fear ends, and that when you emerge from the other side, you're not a courageous person. You're just unafraid. My father taught me that fear is no different than any infinitely deep thing. No different than suffering on a bicycle. No different than shouldering a marriage that's gone to hell because your husband betrayed you. No different than getting lost in the frustration of dealing with your child. No different than shame.

And that ended up being the one thing I wish I could tell my father. I'd tell him a joke.

"Knock-knock, Dad," I'd say. "It's not a pancake."

I pull my fingers away from the brake levers and wrap my hands fully back around the deep curve of the handlebar and yell, "Go now!" I feed myself to the pedals. The bike hums. Natalie screams, "Daaaa-daaa!" And just as she does, our bicycle passes through an invisible barrier and we are floating, free in the deep infinity of our speed. There is no pavement. There is no rattling. There is not even the whistling rush of wind in our ears.

"We're flying!" I shout. We are pure light. Our hearts weigh less than feathers.

When our driveway begins rushing at us on the left side of the road, I sluice the bike across the double yellow line and onto the steep rise of the black strip of asphalt, and we rocket up and over the hump and all the way down to our garage. I brake us to a stop, unclip my left foot, and put it down, tipping the bike in that same direction as I do so. I feel the tow-bike jiggle, then hear Natalie's foot hit the blacktop. I swing my right leg over the bike, turn, and look at my daughter.

She is wearing blue sweatpants and a red hoodie with a dog on the chest. Her baby blue, flowered helmet is tilted to the left, giving the intimation that she's tipping her head for a photo. Strands of her hair are spraying out from the edges of the helmet and through the vent holes. Her eyes are wide, wet from the wind, lit by sunlight and adrenaline. She's smiling as if we just saw something funny we should not acknowledge, but are secretly sharing.

I wing my hand at her. She raises hers and meets my palm for a slap muted by our bike gloves.

"Oh Dadda," she says. "Have you ever gone that fast before?"

"Yeah, Boo," I say. "But never with my daughter."

"I was scared and happy."

"Yeah." I look at her. I bend my knees and squat, bringing our eyes level. "Hey, you know," I say, "remember I didn't score ten points last year?"

"I know. You scored four."

"I tried as hard as I could."

"Okay."

"There were a lot of people faster than me." World champions! I could add. Olympic medalists and pros! I could shout. I say, "There were sixty-one men who scored more points than me. And two women."

"Okay."

"The Animal scored three hundred and seventy-two points."

"Okay, Daddy. Do you want to color?"

At the kitchen table, with an explosion of crayons between us, we draw on large sheets of artist's paper, heavy stock that holds the wax and adds a sophisticated texture our simple figures of cats and dogs don't merit. Natalie's picture is better than mine, more vibrant and less forced. She's already a more accomplished artist than either me or Beth, with an instinct for color and, as one of her art teachers said, "great brush control, assured strokes, and a natural flow." But she has inherited Beth's sense of order, which irritates me. Natalie likes to color inside the lines, even when they're lines of her own creation and she could make new ones.

I scribble wildly, bleeding my clash of hues beyond the skins of the animals I've drawn.

"Daddy. Not like that," Natalie says. "You can only do that if you're drawing fur."

"It's fun to go outside the lines," I say.

"No," says Natalie. "It's not good."

"It is," I say. "You can't tell me what's good for me."

"It isn't good," says Natalie, chewing on her lip and studying a kitten she's neatly saturating with purple.

"It is," I say.

"Isn't."

"Look." I pick up a black crayon and scrawl it across the breadth of my paper. "I'll draw what I want. And cats aren't purple." And in that instant when I realize I've lost control, I'm as happy as I've ever been. We color, quiet except for the scratching of our crayons, and we are annoyed with each other, just like real people, and I am so goddamn grateful that I can be annoyed with my daughter that I want to cry.

"Daddy."

"What is it?" I say.

"We weren't really flying."

I set my crayon down and look at her. She is watching me, that thing that is her in her eyes, that thing that is her that is me and Beth. I say, "No."

"It didn't feel like flying, not really, Daddy."

"I know," I say.

"We were just riding a bike, huh, Daddy?"

"Yeah," I say. "That's all we were doing, beautiful girl. We were just riding a bicycle."